The Last Sunrise

A True Story

**Biography of a Ten-Year Old Boy
In Nazi Concentration Camps
During World War Two**

by

Harold Gordon

H&J Publishing Inc.
P.O. Box 2253
Salinas, Calif. 93902-2253
Phone (408) 422 7360
Fax   (408) 422 4098

Library of Congress Catalog Card Number 92-090246
Hard Cover ISBN 0-9632589-0-7
Soft Cover ISBN 0-9632589-1-5
SAN   297 7125

First Printed 1992

Illustration Drawing by: Roberto Lupetti

Cover Design, Art, by: Javier Montiel

H&J Pubslishing Inc.
P.O. Box 2253
Salinas, Calif. 93902-2253
Phone (408) 422 7360
Fax   (408) 422 4099

Manufactured in the United States

Born in the year 1931 in Grodno, Poland and condemned to DEATH at the tender age of ten by Hitler and his Nazis. To be gassed and burned in the gas chambers and crematoriums of such Death—Camps as Auschwitz and others.

Already at the Open Gates of the Gas Chamber of Auschwitz, only feet away from the final doors of no return at the undressing room, when the Sword Of Death was lifted from my throat by the Greatest Power we all know and Call "Our God".

I was that little boy—more than (52) years ago. I feel compelled to tell this story for all who died at the hands of the Nazis and can speak no more. I hope to show an example to others that a person can prevail and live a productive life even though one has suffered and been ruthlessly abused at the hands of others.

Acknowledgements

I wish to extend credit and thanks to the following who have helped in many ways to make this book possible.

First, I want to thank the brave American soldiers who passed my way only three days before the war ended.

Second, my deepest gratitude and thanks to the United States Government for allowing me the privilege of entering this great land.

Third, my thanks to my wife of 41 years, Joyce, who has patiently listened to all my stories and worked with me in this endeavor.

Much gratitude to my sons Steven and David for their encouragement and support in this trying effort.

Last but not least my thanks to loving relatives and many friends who have contributed in various ways to the completion of this book.

Preface

It is not the intention of the author to describe the events of World War Two in great detail and with great accuracy. Neither is it intended to blame the German people for the atrocities that the Nazis committed against the Jewish people and others that died or suffered during those war years.

This is a true story of a ten-year-old boy who found himself hunted for no reason other than being born Jewish and living on the wrong continent, at the wrong time. Little by little, he found himself devoid of friends and relatives—the Nazis took them all. Only a few of the names have been changed.

This is the story of a Jewish boy who grew up in Nazi concentration camps as a political prisoner marked for death, as an enemy of the state, and lived to tell his story.

This is not a book by a defeated person seeking sympathy; rather it is to demonstrate to others that despite adverse living conditions, deprived of a childhood for more than four and a half years while imprisoned in Nazi concentration camps, one can prevail and live to tell his story.

Table of Contents

Chapter 1

Grodno, Poland, 1939

It happened so long ago. Had I not forced myself with all my mental strength to imprint upon my very young mind these thoughts which I'm about to put down in print, they would have vanished from my memory long ago, like the dust from the prairie. Watching the mini series "War and Remembrance" from a comfortable easy chair made it almost impossible for me to believe that I was there and saw, felt, and smelled the odors of war and the systematic extermination of innocent peoples. Instead of harboring hatred and resentment, I have chosen to make my life of value by striving for a good marriage, raising two wonderful sons and building a business. I put my story on hold until the time was right.

Now, some 53 years later, our sons grown and on their own, I am beginning to think about retiring and traveling with my wife of 41 years. But first I must tell my story.

I am aware that there are many good books written by Holocaust survivors, but this is my story, as seen through the eyes of a nine-year-old boy who found himself sentenced to death without the possibility of reprieve, whose only crime was being born Jewish. A boy who, despite Hitler's great might and enormous odds against survival, focused his entire mentality for a period of four and a half years toward a single goal. It required not making one single mistake. Every word and sometimes every breath had to be carefully calculated. It also helped being in the right place at the right time. If I needed help, there was none available; if I needed food, it was nowhere to be found; if I was sick, I had no one to tell.

In spite of the adverse conditions of my childhood during the war years, I have been blessed with good mental and physical health and have provided for my family, for all their economic and emotional needs—not in a lavish way, but we always had enough to eat, clean clothes, and a dry roof over our heads.

I consider myself successful in America. In many Eastern European countries, having food, dry clothing, and a non-leaking roof over your head spells Paradise. When basic human needs are not met, most mental and physical energies are diverted from politics, idealism, and community improvements. Such were the living conditions in the city of Grodno, Poland, where I was born and where my personal story begins.

Grodno was considered a moderately large city, consisting of approximately 60,000 inhabitants, of which one-third were Jewish. It was located at the most northeastern corner of Poland (I say "was located" because it is now part of Russia), on the border of Lithuania on the Niemen River, a large wide river which flowed through the city. Grodno was sometimes referred to as the *Grodner—Guberne*, meaning province or state. Because of its location near the Baltic Sea, it was normal for winter temperatures to reach 40 or more degrees below zero. The countryside was moderately rolling, without any significant hills anywhere on the horizon. The land was mostly inhabited by small family farms using the most primitive farm tools. To the best of my knowledge, there wasn't any mechanical equipment available to farmers. Horses or oxen were all I ever saw attached to a plow. The average altitude was near sea level, and I don't recall water being a problem, at least in my geographic area.

The local farmers were mostly peasants who used to bring their fruits, vegetables, livestock, and poultry to the city market every Friday. Most women did their shopping for the week there. During winter, the same farmers would bring such items as hay, firewood, and leather, to the city to trade.

Grodno was a major railway center with a large railroad station located just north of town having many tracks leading in all directions. We had very few automobiles in the city and even fewer roads to accommodate them. When a motorcycle was parked, it indicated to me that someone was sick in the neighborhood. One of my thrills was to run up to the motorcycle when no one was looking, squeeze the horn–bulb and run away. Squeezing the horn–bulb was great fun, but running away hastily and being confident that no adult was fast enough to catch me was a special delight.

The Niemen river was navigable at places during the summer, but in the winter it would freeze over several feet thick. I recall horses and wagons, loaded with goods crossing the ice. The river was also used for a large skating rink. I remember going ice skating there myself and with my family.

The Niemen was a major part of my life. in addition to ice skating in the winter, my friends and I went fishing and bathing when the weather permitted. During spring and early summer, the river was fast flowing with many whirlpools in its path. When I was only six years old, my father took me down to the river. He rented a kayak with two oars and we went upstream to launch it. We were to float to a small resort called "Lasosna" a few miles downstream. A short while into the trip, my father picked me up, saying "I am going to teach you how to swim," and threw me into the fast—flowing, deep water. I thought for sure that I would drown since I never swam before. I used to just wade in the water when my mother would take me to the beach.

I went under in the rapidly flowing current. My instinct caused me to dog paddle to the surface. I looked up and saw that the current was taking me farther away from the kayak. I was terrified as my father was trying to maneuver closer to me. I grabbed the oar as it swung by me and pulled myself into the kayak. I don't know if this was the day that I learned to swim, but one thing is certain–I have never forgotten that day.

On the left side of the river was a tall bank, and on top was an old palace that belonged to a former Polish Hero named "Pilsutski". I remember reading about him in Polish history. The palace was very well maintained and inside were many former war weapons, such as steel armor suits, swords, cavalry gear, and Polish army uniforms. The floor of polished marble was immaculately maintained. Upon entrance to the palace museum, it was required that shoes be removed. Soft slippers were loaned in order not to mark the shining floor. My brother and I used to like to skid along the floor fast until we hit the wall to stop.

One day at the age of seven, I had a strong desire to go fishing. I borrowed an old bamboo pole from a young friend and got some white thread from my mother's sewing box. I went down to the old slaughterhouse, where I was told there were many large groundworms to be dug. I had an empty shoe polish can in which to store the worms. I even punched a few small air holes in the lid so the worms would have air to breathe. I made a crude fishhook from one of my mother's sewing needles. I also found a two-foot-long piece of string. I attached a small branch to one end for a handle and took it with me in case I caught some fish. I would be able to keep them alive in the shallow cold water by putting a large rock on the stake which was fastened to the string holding the fish until I was ready to go home. I sat there catching little fish and was the happiest kid around, thinking how proud my mother would be of me

5

when she saw what I had done. By the end of the summer day, as the sun was sinking into the river, I was getting ready to go home. I gathered together all my fishing gear and proudly picked up my full string of fish out of the water and with the brightest smile a young boy could wear, I began walking down the beach toward home.

I soon came across a middle-aged neighbor lady who had been sunning on the beach and was also getting ready to go home. She called me by my name, "Hirshel, where did you get those beautiful fish?" I replied, "I caught them myself." She continued, "These are the nicest fish that I have ever seen. Would you like to sell them?" At this point in my life, I had never yet earned one cent and I began to think, "Wouldn't it be nice to earn my own money? I could buy candy with my own earned money. I could give some money to my mother" I thought that Mother might be happier with the cash than the fish. I quickly made up my mind and said, "Sure, that would be fine." The lady on the beach replied, "Would 10 groshens be all right?" Ten groshens was equivalent to ten cents in American money. I said, "Yes, that would be fine."

I could have bought many small candies for five cents and it would still leave five cents for Mother—I could not resist such temptation. The lady began searching through her purse, but could not find any change, only bills came up. She said to me in a very sweet voice, "Would it be all right if I paid you tomorrow?" I replied, "Yes, that would be all right." I knew the lady from the neighborhood and was still overwhelmed with the fact that I was really earning money. Several days later, I had not yet been paid, so I went to the lady's home, knocked on the door, and asked if I could now be paid the ten cents that was owed me. She said, "Yes, just a moment, I will get the money." She returned a few moments later and said, "I am sorry but I couldn't find any, would you mind coming back later when my husband comes home?" I said "yes"—what other choice did I have? I was a child and she was a woman. I didn't want to make her angry, and I left. I returned again several more times and was never able to collect for my fish. I was too embarrassed to tell my mother the story and to admit my stupidity. That was a valuable lesson that I learned at the tender age of seven, one that helped me cope in later years, and a lesson that I will never forget as long as I live.

I recall one main shopping street called "Domnikainski." That street was paved and lined with very nice shops on both sides. The store windows offered nice merchandise such as fur coats, dresses and jewelry. No one I knew ever had enough money to shop there. This street had electric street lights and during the Christmas season the Holiday ornaments were lit and many people would put on their nice clothes and go window shopping. My parents used to take my brother Sender and me walking at night to see all the Christmas decorations. Our parents made us walk well ahead of them because my brother and I wore old hand-me-down clothes that did not fit too well (they were often too large because they came from our older cousins and we had not yet grown into them). Our parents were embarrassed in front of our neighbors.

I lived at 8 Naidusa Street. It was a long narrow street without street lights; it began at Domnikainski and ended about a half mile down into the Jewish sector. During the winter, the street level would rise four to six feet with piled-up snow. We had no snow removal equipment, so the snow would just pile up until it melted in the spring. Sometimes my father would send me down to the bakery on Domnikainski to buy something sweet in the dark winter evenings. I was very scared to go at night with no street lights or flashlight. I used to run as fast as I could toward the lights of Domnikainski and often tripped over a drunken peasant sleeping on the street. I was too proud to admit to anyone that I was scared. I was the older brother and had to set an example.

I lived with my parents in the Jewish sector, which was a self-imposed ghetto. We spoke Yiddish at home and on the street. Most of our friends were Jewish. The shops had Yiddish signs in the windows; the merchants catered to the Jewish trade and we sort of made a living from one another. It was like Chinatown in San Francisco without tourists. Our world consisted of a few square blocks in the ghetto, and outside the ghetto was the Polish sector, a different and strange, unreceptive world to us. From time to time, the Poles would break windows in the home or business of a Jew, or beat up Jewish people.

We felt much safer among our own kind in the ghetto. I went to a Jewish school called "Javna." I remember being sent home from school by my principal with a note to my mother stating that if I did not bring tuition soon I would be expelled. I also remember the sad look on my mother's face when she did not have the money. My father had a barber shop and Mother was a homemaker. We had no savings. At times, Mother would go down to the barber shop in the morning and wait for Dad's first customer. Dad gave her the change he had just collected and she would go to the market to buy some food for that day. If he had a slow day, that meant we didn't eat much that day. Polish was a second language to me. All our other studies were in Yiddish and one class was to learn to read and write Polish. My mother spent the days cleaning, cooking, and mending torn clothes.

The four of us, my father, mother, brother, and I lived in a one-room apartment with a kitchen. We had no electricity or plumbing. There was one public toilet in the courtyard for eight apartments. During the summer, the odor was unbearable and in the winter, it would be freezing. From time to time, the human waste would be pumped out and hauled away to a field for fertilization. We had one cold-water faucet in the courtyard. Water had to be hand-carried to all the apartments. Often during winter, the water pipes would freeze and snow was used instead. The Polish peasants who had wagons or horse sleds would earn extra money by going to the river and cutting ice blocks to sell to people like us to store in our cellars.

9

When the ice was covered with sawdust, it could keep through most of the summer. We needed the ice to help keep dairy products from spoiling too soon.

My Uncle Jake and his wife also lived in the courtyard. His children were all married and lived away from home. He was the uncle who taught me things and he was good natured. In another apartment, where the bakery was located, lived my grandmother Fruma with her youngest daughter Sarah, Sarah's husband David Burder and their little daughter about my age, maybe a year or so younger. David Burder had a small candy factory on the premises. Compared to most, he was well-to-do. I used to go to his candy factory sometimes, even though I was never welcome. My grandmother used to help, wrapping candy by hand. Once in a while when no one was looking, grandmother would slip a few pieces of candy into my hand. If Uncle Burder ever saw me taking a piece of candy, he would chase me and take it away from me. One day, Uncle Burder offered me a piece of what I thought was candy. It was really candy coloring concentrate. I took it from him and put it into my mouth. I immediately got very sick and began vomiting. He laughed at me and said, "It serves you right for sneaking candies."

Sometimes I went to play with my cousin. Her mother used to feed her a soft-boiled egg in an egg holder dish, with bread and butter. I used to watch her push away the egg dish, but her mother forced her to eat. I stood there, starving, hoping that my aunt would offer me some. She never did. My mother couldn't afford to buy me an egg and I knew it. I went home with my hunger pains and no food.

Also in the same apartment with Grandma lived my youngest uncle, Shmoel (who was Sarah's twin brother) with his young wife. Uncle Shmoel had a leather store—not leather goods; he just sold hard leather for soles and soft leather for shoes. He made a living but not enough to have his own apartment.

Our apartment had a loosely nailed wooden floor with quarter-inch spaces between the boards. When we swept the floor, no dust pan was needed. The dirt would just fall into the spaces and be gone. With no heat to keep the apartment dry, mildew was always present. Sanitation was far from good. Yet we were happy—we just didn't know any better and were satisfied to go on living that way.

There was a public bath house located just a few blocks from my home. My uncle Jake would take my brother and me for a bath every Friday. We all did that to get ready for the Friday night Sabbath dinner. When I was very small, I used to go to the mikva with my mother and grandmother. (the *mikva* was a large body of water, somewhat like a small swimming pool). I used to swim in the *mikva* . The Jewish women used to go there for purification for the Sabbath and other religious reasons.

Uncle Jake also lived in our apartment court. He was a handyman and caretaker. He used to take care of the doctor's house when the doctor went on vacation. One day when he was getting ready to go over there, he asked me if I'd like to go with him. I said "Of course—who wouldn't like to see the doctor's house!" We went over there on foot. The doctor lived several miles from us at the better end of town. After we finished the yard work, my uncle took me inside. It was beautifully furnished with heavy French Provincial furniture. The bedrooms were large and the beds were high off the floor. The ceilings were at least ten feet high and the massive furniture complemented the walls. The curtains were of white lace and Persian rugs covered most of the hardwood floors. I had never seen such an elaborate house. The bathroom had a real bathtub with hot and cold running water, a sink with two faucets and a toilet. I had never seen an indoor bathroom before. All pipes were exposed, making it easy to do repairs in the winter. I asked my uncle if I could take a bath and he replied "yes." I filled the bathtub with hot water (that was the first time in my life that I had seen a bathtub). I climbed inside—it was very deep—and then I swam from one end to the other. When I hit the end I could push off with my feet until my head hit the other end of the tub. I will never forget that wonderful experience. I thought I had a good life, never realizing how poor we really were.

There was an old Jewish cemetery at the edge of town, just around the corner from the slaughter-house. The cemetery must have been several hundred years old. Many of the tombstones sank deep into the ground and the names were submerged. Other tombstones sank below the ground surface.

Beyond the cemetery was a deep ravine by a creek, and beyond that was the Gentile quarter.

My grandmother Fruma, on my mother's side had a bakery. My grandfather on my mother's side was called "Hirshy the Baker." He died while my mother was pregnant with me and I was named after him. I was told that he was a very learned man and well respected in the community. When I was introduced to people, they would not call me by name. Instead they would say. "This is Hirshy the Baker's grandson." Then people would know who I was.

My mother had a private tutor come to our home after school about three times a week to teach me Hebrew. She was hoping I would become a rabbi. I would have rather played soccer with my friends but disobeying was out of the question.

My younger brother had a slight heart problem, so it was my responsibility to look after him. It meant not running too fast with my friends or paddling too hard in the water. He was 13 months my junior and we were very close. We had to be to protect ourselves from some of the Polish children who would call us "dirty Jews." The environment outside the ghetto was not receptive to us. It was like living in a strange land and not knowing when the time would come for us to get out. We knew from past history that sooner or later the Cossacks or others like them would come, cause pogroms and destroy Jewish property and even hurt and kill us.

On Friday night, we all would gather for the Sabbath dinner. At sundown Grandma would sing for all her grandchildren. She had a very nice singing voice and she would continue singing until we fell asleep. On Sabbath, a Polish friend would come to light our ovens. It was against our religion for us to start a fire on the Sabbath.

Two blocks up, around the left corner, in a small upstairs apartment, lived my paternal grandparents. My grandfather, Fishel, was a tailor by trade; therefore he was called "Fishel der Schneider", which translated means "Fishel the Tailor". My grandmother Rivka was a homemaker. My father's family were non-believers; they ate pork, and did not observe the Sabbath. In contrast, my mother's family were very religious, Orthodox Jews, and very well respected in the community. My father's marriage to my mother created quite a rift in the families.

My mother had 10 or 11 brothers and sisters, and on my father's side there were an equal amount. During the early 1900s, some of the oldest brothers and sisters of both families managed to emigrate to America and Palestine. After they settled and found work, they eventually brought their families over.

From my mother's side, two of her oldest brothers Joshua and Label, (whom I had never met) migrated to Palestine with their wives and later raised families. The younger ones never had a chance to emigrate. On my father's side, his older brother "Zelik" (who later was instrumental in bringing me to America) migrated to Los Angeles, California, and a year and six months later, after he was settled, he brought over his wife Lakie and their six-year-old son. Father's oldest sister, Shainke, was fortunate to move to Stockholm, Sweden, where they raised a son and daughter. My father's youngest brother, Label and his young bride Betty escaped to Buenos Aires, Argentina, where they also raised a family and suffered under the dictatorship of the Péron era.

I recall an incident when my grandfather Fishel obtained an old Singer foot-operated sewing machine. All the local tailors assembled in front of his apartment and wanted to destroy the sewing machine. They shouted that this contraption would put all the tailors out of work. Luckily they were unsuccessful and the sewing machine remained. Later, others began obtaining sewing machines and there was enough work for everybody.

Another rather unpleasant incident I recall was when my father's youngest sister was going to marry a tailor. My grandfather wanted to give the old Singer sewing machine to his youngest daughter for a wedding present so her new husband could get a better start. Father's middle brother, Shike, wanted the sewing machine for himself because he was also a tailor and because of his birthright,—being older, he felt he should be the recipient of "any substantial inheritances or gifts". My father argued that he (Shike) was already established and that Fishel's wish was to be honored. My uncle Shike grabbed a butcher knife and rushed toward Dad shouting, "I am going to kill you for this." My father ran out of range and the large kitchen table stood between them. I watched in horror and disbelief as Shike was trying to kill my father. After a while, Father managed to convince him that it was their youngest sister that was being helped, and he agreed and put the knife down.

My father Ely employed two barbers in his shop. I often was sent by my mother to his barber shop to see if he could bring home some change for groceries. Father also did ladies' hair. His barber shop was always closed on Sundays, not because he wanted the day off but rather because it was against the law to do business on Sunday. Poland is a predominantly Catholic country, and church and state were not necessarily separate. Even though it was forbidden to work on Sundays, Dad had a few of his regular customers come over to his barber shop on Sunday mornings. He'd let them in the back door and then cut their hair. I sometimes watched through the crack in the front door for a possible informer. The punishment was severe. On Saturdays, he'd let me help out by sweeping the floor, taking out trash, and by doing other jobs. For my efforts at the barber shop, Father arranged to have the local shoemaker make me a new pair of sandals. Within a week, I had the new sandals on my feet. These were the first new shoes I had ever owned; I was very proud to wear them.

One of my favorite things to do, a very special treat, was to go to a movie. I used to like Charlie Chaplin movies (I still do). Tarzan movies were quite a thrill, too. In school, it was my favorite topic of conversation with my friends. Swinging from a vine in the jungle and fighting alligators were the ultimate fantasies to a young boy.

My other favorite things to do were to walk along the riverbank toward Lasosna. Lasosna was a small vacation area where people would go for a few days to get away from the city. There was a very nice forest with many large, evenly spaced pine trees. The ground was thickly littered with pine needles and leaves. There were some old cabins available for rent, and the shady area provided by the pine canopy offered great relief from the hot summer sun.

One Sunday as I made my way along the river bank to Lasosna I reached the forest and began running among the pine trees. I came across a few older boys I knew from school who were trying to climb a tall pine tree. They were struggling and not doing that well. One of the boys said to me, "Can you climb that tall tree?" I replied, "Of course I can." The older boy said, "I'll bet you 25 groshens that you can't." While one of the other boys held the 25 groshens bet, I quickly removed my new sandals and rushed toward the pine tree. I began climbing confidently toward the very top. I was making excellent progress and figured I would soon be 25 groshens richer. I was sure that I would win that bet because I was a good climber and would never bet on anything that I wasn't sure I could win. Once more I felt the exuberance of having 25 groshens in my pocket to do with as I pleased. I reached the top of the tree in no time and looked down. To my amazement, the boys were gone and so were my brand new sandals.

Horror struck me. What do I do now? How can I come home without my new sandals? My father will kill me! I sat there at the top of the pine tree and cried. I couldn't stay there forever, so I descended to the ground, still not believing what had happened to me. I tried to think up a story which would be believable, that would be less stupid than what actually happened, but I couldn't think of anything good. I tried to think of something that would appear not to be my fault. But how does one explain sandals disappearing from one's feet? I decided to go home and tell the truth. I was clearly aware, knowing my father, that the truth would be very painful.

I walked barefoot all the way home and tried to enter the house as unobtrusively as I could. My father noticed immediately that my sandals were missing. He shouted to me, "Where are your sandals?" I did not reply. Again he shouted at me, but this time in a louder voice, "What did you do with your new sandals?" I ran over to my mother for protection, but that did not stop my father. He came over and demanded that I tell the whole story, which I did.

I noticed my father's anger growing in his eyes. He shouted, "How can anyone be so stupid, how can you be so irresponsible?" I understood my father's anger. Shoes were very hard to come by and expensive. He was more than a little disappointed in me and I felt it. He began to unbuckle his belt and I knew what that meant. He removed the belt from his trousers, yanked me away from the protection of my mother, pulled my pants down, laid me across his lap

18

and began swinging his leather strap across my bottom.

The whacks were hard and painful. I felt that I could handle a few and not give in to tears, but with each whack the pain increased until it was unbearable and I began to scream. My mother could not stand it any longer. She rushed over to me and yanked me away from my father. I ran as fast as I could, pulling up my pants as I was running, to Grandma's house. My grandma Fruma was always very nice to me and I really loved her a lot. She gave me a few candies and said some comforting words to make me feel better. That was another hard lesson for a nine-year-old boy to learn.

Uncles, Aunts, Cousins. I had many more relatives not shown on this photo.

My Father seated on the left, Mother standing next to Dad, my Brother only (9) months old on Grandma's lap. I am sitting on my Father's lap with a toy wooden horse in my hands. This photo was given to me by my Uncle Julius who lived in America.

Why was I spared ?

Chapter 2

Grodno Under Russian Rule

It was Friday afternoon on September 1, 1939. We heard some planes up high in the sky. I had never seen any planes before then. A few minutes later, we heard some more planes and we could see them now. They began diving and dropping bombs. There were bombs exploding and fires erupting in some parts of the city. Most people had no idea what was happening. No one imagined that World War Two was beginning. The attack was totally unexpected and, by the next day, German tanks and artillery were at the outskirts of our city. We all panicked and were totally unprepared for what was to follow. The advancing German units reached the west banks of the Niemen River. They waited for additional units to catch up and make the crossing. Several days later, we were surprised to find that they had not yet attempted to cross the Niemen.

We learned later that the Russian advancing units had also marched into Poland from the east. A non-aggression pact was made between Germany and Russia to partition Poland. Russia was to occupy the eastern half and Germany would take the rest. Fortunately for me, my city was to be occupied by the Russians. All ears were glued to the radio and every country broadcast a different version of the news. I was terrified. I heard people saying that the Germans put Jews in ghettos and took away their homes and belongings. I asked my mother if that was true. She replied, "No, it is not true." She did not want to worry my brother and me. I could sense that she was trying to protect us from the dreadful news and the bad times which were upon us.

The Polish army completely disintegrated and the Polish soldiers began disposing of their uniforms. The cavalry horses were abandoned and the farmers gathered them to help plow the fields. The city was without law and order. People began looting the stores, particularly hoarding food. The city officials went into hiding and everything came to a halt.

News came that the Russians had crossed the borders and were advancing. I did not fear the Russians because we were so poor that there was nothing they could take from us. I heard the elders talking about the Cossacks and how they would have pogroms and hurt the Jews when they got drunk. I became alert to sudden change and dangers.

I was born on January 1, 1931, and I was now an adult (mentally at least) before my ninth birthday. My childhood had ended. To face the challenges which lie ahead, I had to think quickly—that was my instinct if I was to survive.

The weather turned cold much earlier that year. The freezing raindrops landing on my face caused great pain. The leaves from the trees were almost all gone because winter was setting in. My father began more aggressively to trade with the peasants for supplies of food to be stored for the long winter and beyond. Since my grandmother owned a bakery, she accumulated many sacks of flour for making bread. We knew that storing enough food would be our greatest challenge.

Russian tanks and advance units entered the city in a big victory parade. There was no fight with the Polish army. My uncle, (David Burder), who was always very sick with stomach ulcers and who never fired a gun, was taken prisoner by the Russians and sent to Siberia. That saved his life, as I will explain later. We welcomed the Russians. We felt that living conditions would eventually improve. We heard that everyone was equal and that everyone had work and food. What could be better than that?

Before the war, a small Communist party existed in Grodno. Some of the Communists were of the Jewish faith. They were under the illusion that if the small amount of wealth that existed in Poland was distributed evenly everyone would become prosperous. The first thing the Russians did was to release all political prisoners. The incarcerated Communists, who spent many years suffering in Polish prisons for their beliefs felt that the Russians would honor them, send them to Russia, and offer them good posts within the government. On the contrary, when they revealed themselves to the Soviets and told of their suffering for the cause, the officials replied, "No, we don't need you in Russia. We have many Communists there already. Stay here in Poland and help raise the living standards." Disillusioned, they reflected on the many years already spent in the Polish prisons pursuing a make-believe dream.

The city of Grodno swelled with Soviet personnel, armaments, and support vehicles. Shortly thereafter, the bureaucrats and their families began arriving to form new local and regional governments, and all private property was immediately confiscated, becoming the property of the state. My father's barber shop was seized and he became an employee in his own shop. He and the other two barbers in the shop had to pay rent and a portion of the gross to an agency of the Soviet government. All the barbers shared equally the little money remaining after expenses .

The currency changed from "zlotys" (Polish money) to "rubles" (Soviet money). Of course, everyone was suddenly without funds as the Polish zlotys became worthless overnight. My family had no measurable amount of Polish currency, so it made little difference to us, but people with money suddenly became poor and everyone became equal at this point. Homeowners became renters of the state, as all homeowners lost legal title to their dwellings. Frequently, if only one or two people lived in a large home, the Soviet Housing Authority would assign additional people to live with them. Suddenly, homeowners found themselves living with many strangers in what used to be their own home.

As in all wars, consumer goods are the first to disappear. All the stores and shops were empty because of looting and hoarding by local residents. Whenever basic food supplies became available for distribution, long lines formed immediately. There were never enough supplies for all the people in line. Often when a rumor was heard that a certain store would have supplies, my mother would send me to hold a place in line in the event it was true. Often the rumor was false and the long hours in line were wasted.

My grandmother was a smart business woman. She had the foresight to store many sacks of flour in her bakery. We were able to share our good fortune with friends and relatives. In order to earn rubles and kopecks for immediate use, my father began cutting hair for the Russian soldiers. I felt less threatened as a Jew at this time because the Jewish people were tolerated better by the Russians than by the Poles.

Schools were set up and all children of school age were required to attend classes six days a week. We even had to go to school on Saturdays. As I mentioned earlier, my mother was very orthodox, and going to school on Saturday was a sin. It was the Sabbath and a day of rest. My mother asked my father to go to the school principal, who was a Russian, to persuade him to make an exception, and allow me to be absent on Saturdays. To my amazement, the principal must have been sympathetic to the Jewish people and agreed to my father's request. The only stipulation was that I would keep up with the class and receive good grades. My father and I gladly agreed to such a lenient request and walked home to inform Mother.

The teachers were Russian, and all subjects were taught in Russian. Maybe because of my very young age, the Russian language came quite easily to me. It is similar to Polish and I became fluent in it in a very short time. I was even helping my parents learn it. I made some Russian friends (children of the officials that were sent over from Russia to set up the new government and the schools). I spent a lot of time with my new young friends, with whom I felt equal. They treated me like any other child on the block. Because we were poor before the war, our transition to communism made us more acceptable to the Russians.

The hard Nordic winter had us in its grip. The countryside was covered with a thick, crisp layer of snow. All the trees were bare. They appeared dead, silhouetted against the white snow. All the houses had their windows boarded up to conserve heat. The animals were in their barns. Very little movement was observed on the streets of Grodno during the winters. Just walking to school only a few short blocks was enough to get frostbite. My mother used to bundle me up the best she could before sending me to school. In addition to warm clothing, I wore a wool hat, earmuffs, and heavy gloves. By the time I arrived at school, my extremities were numb and blue. We had no electric heater or gas furnaces at school. The only source of heat available in our school room was a small coal—burning stove in the middle of the room. There was barely enough coal to get a very small fire going.

The Russians were accustomed to cold winters and brought felt boots along with them to Grodno. These boots were not waterproof and would not keep out the slush. During hard cold winters, when the ice was frozen solid and the snow was crisp and powdery, they were excellent to keep out the cold. The size didn't matter. I learned from the Russian soldiers to wrap rags around my feet to fill the empty space in my boots if they were too large. The result was comfortable, dry and warm feet.

I made friends with a Russian boy in my class. His father was a "Commissar" in the Russian army.

That meant he was an officer. The boy's name was Gregory. When Gregory got a new pair of skis for his birthday, my father was able to purchase the old skis from his father for my brother and me. Often we went skiing together. When my younger brother tagged along, he and I would skate on one ski each. We never even thought it was odd. It was the natural thing to do.

Once there was a ski race in our school. The whole class was taken on an outing in a horse drawn sled to a small hill where we were to have our ski race. We all mounted our skis and began the race. About halfway down the hill, both my skis came off my shoes and I began tumbling in the deep snow. I finally came to rest at the bottom, and by the time I gathered my skis and ski poles together the race was over. I cried and was saddened by my unfortunate experience. We returned to our classroom, and after the skis had thawed I noticed that both leather straps that held the skies securely to my shoes had been cut about three-quarters of the width. I became even more hurt and came home crying, informing my father of what had happened. Someone had sabotaged my skis and caused me to become disqualified. My father took me by the hand and said, "Grab your skis, we are going back to school to see the principal." I was grateful for my father's support in this matter and quickly followed him. My father complained to the principal about the unfairness and cruelty done to me. The principal was very sympathetic but the guilty boy was never found. It made me feel much better having my father stand up for me. There had already been several disappointments in my childhood and a little support from my dad was something I really needed.

One Sunday morning, my friend Gregory came by my house and asked me to go ice skating with him. (I owned a pair of old ice skates that belonged to my cousin. They were quite rusty and the skating edge was not very sharp.) I said "Yes I would like that," and we went down to the river where the ice was frozen solid many feet thick. We saw many people ice skating. Horses and wagons were crossing in several places. It was amazing to me that a river that was so swiftly flowing in the summer could become frozen so solid in the winter. The frozen surface was so large that one could ice skate for hours in one direction. It was a winter Paradise.

I remember the fun things we did, maybe because they were so few. One clear cold evening, just before Christmas while all the holiday decorations were displayed beautifully on Stalin Street (once known as Domnikainski), my father took my mother, brother, and me for a sleigh ride. He hired a horse sled complete with driver, jingle bells, and blankets. We all snuggled up under the heavy blankets and had the most joyous sleigh ride on that crisp, starlit night.

My household chores increased measurably in the winter. In addition to chopping and bringing up firewood, I had to keep the house supplied with water. It meant taking two pails at one time down a few blocks to a water well that wasn't frozen. I would attach the pail to a hook at the end of a heavy rope. Then I would turn the crank to lower the pail to the bottom of the well and try to scoop up some water.

(Once I lost the pail in the well. It became disengaged from the hook and went under.) Then the trick was to carry both pails of water over the slippery streets of ice and snow without spilling most of it. Usually by the time I reached home, the pails were half empty.

Unknown to me at that time, the Soviets began indoctrinating the young people into the communist party. I must have been in the third or fourth grade when a party member visited our school, gave us all red scarves and pins, and called us "young pioneers." Once a week he would conduct a class on party ideology and make us feel important. I had no idea what the red scarf meant, and it was a good thing that I didn't.

I was progressing very well with my Hebrew studies. Mother wanted me to become a rabbi or a scholar like my grandfather. I was also beginning to prepare for my bar mitzvah. Learning was a major part of our lives. The alternative to learning was being a bum. That was unacceptable in our family. Books were treasured and teachers were revered. It was my ability and willingness to learn that later was helpful in my struggle for survival.

We thought that this new way of life under Russian rule would go on indefinitely and we were prepared to accept it. Instead, it lasted only about two years. We spent most of our time scrounging for a living, learning the Russian customs and language. We continued to preserve our cultural and religious heritage. We were not permitted to travel, but that was no problem because we had never traveled in the past. The entire world known to me physically was within a mile radius. Anything beyond that was inconceivable to me.

I recall an amusing story told by the elders in my family. It was about one of my father's brothers. He was invited to dinner to meet a young lady in a nearby village, about ten miles out of town. When he returned, his mother and father asked, "How did you like her?" His reply was, "Well, she wasn't very pretty, but I had a nice Sabbath dinner at her house and I feel obligated to marry her." He did marry the young lady and they had many children.

I felt sad for the Jewish people who lived in the western part of Poland under German occupation. We knew that life was more difficult for them. On the other hand, I took comfort in the fact that I lived under Soviet occupation and did not fear for my life. I also felt somewhat more secure since we all knew that Germany and Russia signed a non-aggression pact when Poland was partitioned between the two countries.

The intellectuals who once ruled Poland were removed from their posts and replaced by communists, many of whom had recently been released from political prisons. They had no experience in governing and as a result the population at large suffered. Consumer goods were in very short supply. Trading with the village peasants was about the only way to put food on the table. The winter passed and by summer the standard of living did not improve. There were always bread lines, and any consumer goods that were put on the shelves disappeared in the blink of an eye. It appeared that we would continue living under Russian rule indefinitely and we had resigned ourselves to that fact. My entire family learned to speak Russian. My brother and I even learned to read and write our new language in a very short time.

The months and seasons passed too quickly and I was already two years older. Another major change was about to occur in my life. Our struggle for survival was so intense, and the odds so small, that it took the western world until near the end of the war, May 1945, to believe the truth. Even to this day there are some who will never acknowledge it.

My immediate Family. Father Ely, Mother Bluma, Brother Sender and me, sitting on the little table. Sentenced to Death. Our only crime, "Born Jewish."

Chapter 3

German Troops March on Russia

Suddenly and without warning, Germany attacked Russia with great force and speed. It was on a Sunday, June 22, 1941. The sky became filled with German planes and the Russians were taken by complete surprise. The Russian so-called defense was easily smashed by the rapidly advancing German army. German paratroopers landed in Minsk, to the east of us, and the city fell to the Germans before our town was taken three days later. On the third day, German tanks, personnel carriers, and foot soldiers began arriving in Grodno. By that time, most of the Russian soldiers were either gone or out of uniform. The streets were cleared of people. The Germans would shoot at anyone or anything which moved. I opened the door of my home and walked a few steps to the stairway to take a better look at the German soldiers patrolling the streets. One German soldier noticed my movement, raised his rifle and fired at me. The bullet missed and I quickly returned to the safety of my home.

I remember as my uncle Shmoel was going from one apartment to the other, he was shot at several times. Luckily, he wasn't hit. Any door that was not locked securely was an open invitation to the Germans to come in and take what they wanted. They raped and killed at will. It was, of course, with the consent of the Nazi High Command. The shooting was frightening. The smell of death was in the air and the city's entire population was frozen with fear. As I peeked through a crack in our window shutters, I saw some dead people lying on the street in pools of blood. I had never seen so much blood before and the sight of it made me sick. During the following months, the city became paralyzed as food supplies dwindled.

Prior to age nine, my childhood suddenly ended and I became an adult. There was not to be an adolescent period in my life nor would my education continue. I sensed that there would not be any more playing for me. I had become a man, whether I was ready or not. I saw life, death, and destruction. I was beginning to read faces and to feel the pain and sorrow that others were expressing. I was beginning to learn the meaning of a look or slight gesture, and to respond immediately in an appropriate manner. I didn't have to be told what to do. Observing my parents faces was enough for me to get the message. I was also beginning to learn a new emotion—uncertainty. It was on everyone's face. Previously I had been able to ask my parents anything and get an answer. Asking questions was now useless. It was obvious that no one had any answers. I felt that if I asked any difficult questions my parents would have to either guess or lie to spare me from worrisome knowledge. It was better to just wait and observe.

My brother, Sender, was 13 months my junior. It doesn't seem like much, but at that early age he was still a child and I was the big brother he looked up to for comfort and protection. His slight heart murmur caused him to depend on me more than a younger brother normally would. I loved him very much and it was no bother to me. I felt needed, and that in turn gave me more strength.

The Germans, with the help of former Polish officials began setting up local and regional governments in all the previously government—occupied buildings.

The press was one of the first enterprises which the Germans took over. Almost immediately, posters printed in both Polish and German were distributed all over the city. The local population was most eager to read the posters to learn of any news.

One of the first posters that reached the streets said that all weapons must be turned in immediately. Individuals with weapons beyond a certain date would be punished by death. An official seal appeared on the bottom of all posters: "The German High Command."

People were frightened and most of the guns were turned in. At random and without warning houses were searched for weapons. If some weapons were found the entire household would be shot to death at the city square as an example to others.

Soon after, the presses were rolling again with new orders from the German High Command. "All radios must be turned in at once." Then followed the familiar warning. Any persons not complying would be executed along with their entire family. Shortly thereafter, more house searches, more executions and everyone in our city got the message. There were some who defied the German authorities; they knew the risks they were taking.

Without radios or press, the civilian population had no knowledge of how the war was going. As the months passed, we became paranoid with the total lack of any news. We could only guess by how many trainloads of German soldiers passed though Grodno headed to the Russian front. Counting the trainloads of wounded German soldiers returning from Russia gave us some idea.

Additional German High Command orders followed: "Everyone must register and obtain an identity card." Of course, among other pertinent information requested, was one's religion. We knew the reason for that was to identify all Jews for special treatment later on. What could we do? If we told the truth we were doomed, and if we lied we might be shot now. The next general order that followed was that all Jews must wear a yellow Star of David, three to four inches across, sewn onto clothing and worn on the left side of the chest. Of course, failing to wear a yellow star on the left meant defrauding the Germans. We were well aware of the consequences. Even small children and babies had to wear a yellow Star of David on their clothing. The Jewish people felt singled out and degraded, and thus began the extermination of the Jews of Eastern Poland (not yet known to us or to the rest of the world).

A shadow of darkness and despair closed in on our population at a calculated rate. A little freedom, just a little at a time, was taken away. Not a lot all at once. It seemed to us that giving up a little was not so bad. What we didn't know was that much greater sacrifices were on the horizon.

German forces, with the help of local unpaid labor, began stripping the city of all metals, such as statues, iron gates, wrought iron fences, and whatever raw material was available. It was all shipped to Germany, supposedly to help with the war effort. Grodno began to look barren without all the familiar landmarks. But it was war and with the loss of our freedom and pleasures, this was just one more loss to endure.

The economy became totally disrupted. The Russian rubles became worthless, and Germany began issuing "Occupation Marks" that weren't much better. But what choice did we have? It was either worthless marks or worthless rubles.

We all had to live off the land. All the goods from the shops were gone, stolen either by the former managers, looters, or Germans. In any event, trading with the local farmers for grains, potatoes, vegetables, and poultry was the only way to obtain food. Those who had expensive dishes, tableware, furs, furniture, or any other items such as gold, silver, or diamonds were the first to trade. Later, people began trading services for food. My father was a barber, and even during wartime people needed haircuts and shaves. The disposable razor blade was not yet available to us. Most men had to go to the barber shop for a shave, unless of course, one had and could use a straight-edge razor. My father began cutting hair and shaving people at their homes, on the street or in our small apartment. For his service he would receive such items as a hunk of bread, a piece of cheese, a pat of butter, a cigarette butt, potatoes, and even firewood. My father did not smoke, so he would trade the cigarette for some other item. This method provided food for us and also for our relatives who possessed no special skills. Once, I remember my father went to the village and returned with a wagon of potatoes. He traded one of his suits for the potatoes and managed to borrow a horse and wagon for the delivery.

Never in my youth did I have new clothes, except for my new sandals that did not last very long. I always wore hand—me—downs from my cousins in Israel and Sweden. Fabrics were unavailable and we had to make do with what clothes we had. My mother and grandfather (who was a tailor) helped keep our clothes together, always darning and patching.

The long hard winter was approaching, with temperatures often below 40°. It was time to prepare as usual, but this time was different. There was little to prepare with—no one had much and the consequences were clear. The elderly and the sick would be the first to succumb; small children would follow.

As the months passed, the heavy snows began to pile up on the landscape and the temperature stayed well below freezing for months. As predicted, many epidemics such as tuberculosis, typhoid fever, and dysentery occurred. This time we had no medicine, so the death toll was greater.

Everywhere I looked, I saw German soldiers warmly dressed in their heavy winter clothing, their pointed rifles silhouetted against the white snow. The winter days were short and we were trying to do as much preparation during the daylight hours as possible while dodging the Nazi soldiers. The sky stayed gray most of the time, while the cold, relentless wind blew in from the Baltic. During the long dark evenings, we met at relatives' homes to discuss the events of the day. The children usually just observed and listened intently. Families lived in fear and gathered together.

The German High Command in Berlin was well advanced with its plans for the final solution of the Jews. The plans were in great detail and executed very systematically. I will attempt to tell the way I saw it, to the best of my ability at least, in the following chapters.

On the frozen "Niemen River", my father on ice-skates Mother helping to push "Sled-chair". My brother is sitting in front of Dad. I am next to Mother.

Chapter 4

The Grodno Ghetto

Hitler's elite troops, called SS, arrived on the scene. They were a completely separate segment from the regular German army which operated independently, dealing mainly with internal problems. Their primary missions was identifying and eliminating all political opponents of Hitler and dealing with the final solution of the Jews. To the best of my knowledge, the SS and Gestapo incarcerated and eliminated thousands of known Hitler opponents. That was the main reason the concentration camp "Dachau" was originally built, some 16 miles out of Munich, near the small village of Dachau, Germany.

After the elimination of Hitler opponents (and a large number of Russian prisoners) at Dachau, the SS devoted its entire effort to dealing with the final Jewish solution.

In Grodno, the SS summoned all the Jewish leaders in our community and directed them to form a council. The council was to implement SS orders to the Jewish population at large. Those selected to serve on the council were leaders of the Jewish community. They were the intellectuals, rabbis, educators, etc. These council members were given special passes and arm bands which allowed them to move about more freely and have access to the SS authorities.

One of the first dramatic orders I remember having levied upon us was for all Jews living outside the Jewish sector to move into the Jewish sector for their own protection from the anti-semitic Poles. People had to leave the homes where they had lived all their lives, and leave most of their belongings behind. The Jewish council designated where these people should move to and with whom. Several families had to live in previously single-family apartments.

Shortly after, ten foot brick walls were erected on the streets blocking access from one side of the street to the other. Any windows facing outside the ghetto were filled with bricks and mortar. One street was left where no wall was built. It was to become the main gate to the ghetto.

We were completely encircled by brick wall structures; the only way in and out was through the main gate guarded by SS troops. The council was ordered to form a police force of Jews who carried no weapons—only a club—to enforce whatever the SS considered necessary. They wore white arm bands and a blue Star of David on their left arms. They were stronger and healthier men and some were feared because they felt that by obliging the SS, their quality of life would improve. In some cases it did (for a while). They were given passes to go outside the ghetto to bring in food for their families.

Posters appeared all over the ghetto stating that all Jews must register immediately in order for the German authorities to request sufficient rations to feed the ghetto population. So began the registration of all the Jews in our ghetto, and when it was done we totaled about twenty thousand. Failing to register would result in no food rations.

Food shortages became more critical as the months passed and many people were dying from hunger, disease, and lack of sanitation. Medical supplies were almost non—existent. Vigorous trading over the ghetto fences with the Polish population increased significantly. As the situation became more desperate, we traded whatever we could find for food and wood. Much food passed over the fences. Eagerly, the Jews traded watches and gold rings for a loaf of bread or a chicken. The water was turned on and off at various intervals, causing further confusion.

Hungry, cold, and without sanitation, we began to wonder how long the free world would stand for this and let innocent people be enslaved. We all tried hard to live together in peace, running our small shops and bakeries. Schools were organized for the children. Six months passed as the ghetto population became weaker, both physically and mentally. Hope was nowhere on the horizon. My uncle Shmoel became mentally ill. He kept referring to Jews as dead corpses walking around. He looked at me one day and cried. He said "Hirshel, you are dead." I really became scared. I didn't know what he meant. He meant it was a matter of time before we would all be dead by the hand of the Nazis. Of course, no one at that time believed that was to happen. Later we realized that he wasn't crazy. He had a vision.

The temperature continued to fall below 30° and corpses were accumulating. Work details were formed to collect the dead in wagons and take them outside the ghetto walls to the Jewish cemetery for burial in mass graves. It was considered good luck to be selected for that detail. Going outside the ghetto walls meant being able to trade with the peasant farmers if the German guards permitted. The frozen bodies were as stiff as boards. The ground at the cemetery was frozen many feet deep. Digging the graves was a difficult task, to say the least. The burial detail would return to the ghetto late in the afternoon, weak, tired, and many with frostbite.

Suddenly one day without warning, the gates of the ghetto opened wide and a convoy of several personnel carriers drove into the ghetto, led by the ghetto commander and escorted by a company of SS personnel armed with submachine guns. They shouted, "We need one hundred strong men for a work detail outside the ghetto." Many more volunteered than were needed. As I said earlier, being outside the ghetto meant opportunity. The council had to make the selection and only the strongest and healthiest qualified. By the next day, when the workers had not yet returned from the work detail, the ghetto commander was asked, "Where are those men?" The reply was that they were safe and working out of town. The families of those men were crying and begging for answers, but none were given.

A few days later the SS returned and asked for two hundred more men. We began to resist. I remember an incident right in our court when somebody threw some acid at an SS soldier's face as he came to get some Jews. He was then beaten to death. The next day more SS men with automatic

44

weapons arrived in the ghetto in armored personnel carriers and sealed off the block where the incident took place. They rushed from house to house shouting "Ale Raus!" ("Everyone out!") When all the houses on the block were vacant and all men, women, and children were on the street, in the cold, wearing only what they had on when the SS arrived that early morning, the SS went from house to house searching for more people. Anyone found hiding was forced into the freezing street. Even the elderly and the bedridden people were removed from the houses. The SS men lined up on the sidewalk facing the civilian people lined up in the middle of the street and opened fire. The blasting from the submachine guns was terrifying. As we looked out the window from the next block, we saw people lying dead in pools of red blood, contrasted against the white snow. It was a horrible sight. The SS soldiers boarded the waiting vehicles and drove out through the main gate as though nothing had happened, leaving the dead in the middle of the street where they had stood alive just moments before. My mother tried to prevent my brother and me from viewing this horrible incident. It was too late. The scene has been imprinted in my brain, and I can never forget it.

There were some militant Jews who said, "We are not going to take this; we are going to kill some more Germans." They killed three German soldiers with knives. The following day, more SS personnel arrived in armored personnel carriers. They went from house to house and removed about one hundred more men, women, and children to the

45

street and did the same thing—shot them all in the street for the rest of us to watch. I remember all the elderly screaming and crying and being almost out of their minds. The sight of their relatives and friends being shot to death in front of their eyes was traumatic, to say the least. The sorrow and grief of the observers must surely have been heard in Heaven above, if such a place exists. The relatives of victims blamed the militant Jews for their relatives' executions. The Jews who retaliated felt that it was hopeless to continue because it wasn't one for one. The SS did not bother to find and punish the responsible parties. The militants did not mind risking their own lives while fighting Germans, but did not want a hundred innocent people to die for their deeds. After that last incident, we sort of gave up and obeyed like sheep. I am sure that these tactics were not unique to our community. The SS had plenty of experience in other communities and they knew that this method worked.

The hard winter finally ended and the ice and snow began to thaw. Springtime was always beautiful in Poland. The contrast between the cold and the freshness of spring was very dramatic. There was lots of moisture from the melting snow and the vegetation grew vigorously, bathed by the warm sun rays and nurtured by the rich, moist soil. Birds appeared, singing in the branches of the trees. Animals such as foxes and wolves emerged from their dens, but it wasn't for our eyes to see them anymore. The animals were still free. We were now the ones that were locked up in a cage!

The pleasant mild temperature of spring never lasted long and soon the hot summer arrived. Living conditions continued to deteriorate. We felt like fish in a barrel where the water of the barrel was evaporating.

One year had passed since the ghetto was established and it was winter again. As a population, we were much weaker in every respect. Many of the elderly had died and some children were born in the ghetto during the year. We had already used up most of our resources and no relief was at hand. By this time, many smaller eastern Jewish communities had been wiped out by firing squads; extermination camps like Treblinka, Auschwitz, Buchenwald, and others were in full operation, although still unknown to us. It was time for the Grodno ghetto Jews to go up in smoke.

A great number of SS troops arrived in our ghetto very early one morning, just before dawn, blocking off a street. A vehicle equipped with loudspeakers drove up and down the street making the following, all—too—familiar announcement: "Everyone out, you are going to Germany to work in factories. Everything you need will be there, so just take what you can carry." Like fools, we still believed that the SS told the truth. We thought they wanted us to work in their factories as slave labor to help them with the war effort. Why would they kill us? What good would we be to them dead? That was our reasoning. It made no sense to kill us. Our reasoning was wrong, of course.

The first group of our people, about two thousand of them, were marched out of the ghetto,

47

and formed what was called a transport. Streets were lined with armed guards on both sides of the column, spaced about 25 feet apart, making escape almost impossible. The ghetto gate closed behind them and they were gone forever. The empty streets and houses left behind were quickly sealed off by Polish crews and the ghetto became smaller. The Polish crews went through all the empty houses and removed all the belongings into the middle of the street. Later, everything was loaded onto trucks and hauled to the railroad station, where it was loaded into boxcars and shipped to Germany. I used to peek through a crack in the fence and see the streets piled high with furniture and clothing. Every time the SS were ready for another transport of people, the same thing happened. The Polish crews would come in and remove all the personal property into the street. Everything would be hauled away, leaving a ghost town behind where just days before a form of human life existed.

In just two months time, our ghetto's population of 20,000 was reduced to half the original size. We knew that our turn was not too far off and we felt trapped, not knowing what we could do. The only comfort left to us was praying to God, hoping that surely He would hear our cries and see our destruction. Our God couldn't continue watching His chosen people being destroyed. Surely a miracle would occur soon. Those were our thoughts. Clinging together with family was a great comfort also. My grandmother Fruma was the strongest, I believe. She was a smart business woman, running the bakery while my grandfather prayed in the synagogue all day. Although my grandfather died 11 years before, Grandmother continued running the bakery. She was responsible for holding the family together at these trying times. She was a woman of wisdom and great hope. She kept reassuring us that everything would turn out well and we had confidence in her.

My grandfather, dad's father, came to live with us in the ghetto. My grandmother had died and he needed a place to stay. He was a non–religious Jew who ate non—kosher food and did not observe our Jewish customs. I remember my mother getting very upset with him because he would bring non–kosher food into our home. He disturbed her terribly. Grandfather finally moved in with my uncle, Father's younger brother Shike. Grandfather was a tailor, so while he lived with us he made my brother and me new clothes from old materials. I liked having him around. He didn't like living with uncle Shike. Grandfather remarried at the age of 80 and he and his new wife moved into a small one—room apartment. She was about his age.

At the next transport, my grandfather and his wife were taken away. They lived in a different part of the ghetto. There was nothing we could do about it. They, along with 2,000 others, were removed in the middle of the night. In the morning when we woke up, they were gone.

One Sunday morning, as I was playing soccer with one of my friends on the street, I saw German troop-carriers loaded with armed SS troops arrive briskly at our street. The SS soldiers unloaded quickly and began going from house to house looking for men. I quickly ran up the stairs to our second—floor apartment and warned my father. The SS were not far behind me. My father quickly jumped out a rear window onto a lower roof and escaped on foot. When the SS got to our apartment they found only my mother, my ten-year-old brother, and me. Their loaded submachine guns, with their fingers on the triggers, looked big and scary. They asked Mother, "Are there any men here?" Mother replied, "No." Then they searched the apartment and left. My heart was pounding with fear. We were afraid if they caught my father they would kill him. Losing my father then meant no chance for survival for the rest of the family. I was so relieved he got away. After the raid was over and the SS left the ghetto, Dad returned home. We were happy to see him return.

Every time a transport of several thousand people departed the ghetto, the remaining people felt secure for at least five days. It took that long for the train to deliver the people and return to Grodno.

Two young men who were taken on a previous transport to Treblinka, and later escaped, returned to the ghetto. They told us a horror story. The transports were being taken to Treblinka and everyone was killed, except for a few who were taken for temporary replacements. They mentioned names of relatives they saw die at Treblinka. Even then, their story was unbelievable and most people regarded it as a lie. We just couldn't believe it. It made no sense, but their story was true!

Although our ultimate destruction was imminent, there was a slight hope that somehow some of us would survive and eventually return to our homes. There was a large open space right above the large oven of my grandmothers bakery. Everyone in our family gathered all their best and most valuable assets to hide there from the Germans and Poles until such time as some returned. Uncle Yudel, (mother's brother) found an old metal bathtub and everyone put their valuables into it. There were linens, silver candle sticks that were in the family for many generations, some jewelry, watches, fur coats, etc. My mother had an old Persian lamb coat which she treasured and which had been handed down for generations. It also was placed in the metal bathtub for hiding. With the help of others in the family, the full bathtub was lifted above the oven and the space was sealed with mortar and bricks. When finished, it was whitewashed and looked like part of the original wall.

Until now, we watched others leave the ghetto in transports. We looked out our windows and saw the unfortunate people being taken away. We recognized many and felt a small comfort that we had not been taken. We knew that our turn would soon come. How would we cope with it? Suppose it was true that the people in the previous transports were taken to their death. That meant that we only had a few days to live. And if we only had a few days to live, how should we spend the remaining days of our lives? How does an eleven-year-old boy make such a decision? How does anyone make such a decision? How many of us ever had to even consider this?

As the temperature dropped, the cold weather continued to take its toll. None of the apartments had any heat. Most anything that would burn was already consumed by the small fires of our wood burning stoves. We always slept with our clothes on. One reason was for warmth and the other was in case we were taken away in the middle of the night with no time to dress. The four of us, mother, father, brother, and I, snuggled up together in one bed. My brother and I were placed between our parents for security and warmth. Also, we had no bathroom in our apartment. We had to go outside in the courtyard to the outdoor toilet, which was no more than a frozen open pit. Being already dressed made the chore easier.

One night, in the early morning hours, we heard trucks arriving in the ghetto. We had heard them many times before, but this time the sound of the engine was louder as if they were on our street. My father got up to look, and sure enough, many trucks filled our street and German soldiers with guns in their arms began disembarking. Father said it looked as though our turn had come. We all began to cry and sob. We quickly realized that we must act, and began to put on us as much clothing as we could. We knew that we would never see our homes again; the more we wore, the less we would carry. That was our reasoning. We began packing our bags with what little we had left to carry with us. We made our bags as heavy as we could possibly carry. My bag was even too heavy for me, but I thought I'd try it anyway. As we were getting ready we heard shouting "Raus," everyone out. That phrase was all too familiar to us. The soldiers entered, emptied the houses, and forced everyone to assemble on the freezing street. The Germans wore heavy protective clothing, long overcoats, leather boots, and leather gloves with their fingers on the triggers of the loaded submachine guns. The elderly and the sick were also forced into the cold, snow-covered street. The wind was howling as the sun began rising in the eastern sky. The wind-chill factor must have been around 50° below or more.

An hour had passed since we left our home and the chill in the cold air had already penetrated our bones. We almost wished that we would leave, if only to keep from freezing. We waited as we were counted several times, both by the local Jewish police and by the Germans. We also had to wait until all the houses were searched to insure that no one remained behind.

We were assembled into a column several hundred feet long and five people deep. A voice shouted, "Turn right and begin marching." The 2,000-person column was surrounded by heavily armed German guards with weapons pointed at us from all directions. We began to move slowly toward the main gate of the ghetto. We were joined by other columns from other streets, now totaling about 3,000 Jews. The column extended for a mile, maybe more. The SS marched alongside of us, spaced about 30 feet apart, making escape impossible. Some of the Jewish people peered out their window, looking for relatives. Most of my relatives were included in this column. We all lived in very close proximity, as mentioned earlier—all my aunts, uncles, cousins, and grandmother. As we walked, the powdery snow crackling beneath our feet, we sensed that we would never again return. My family and I were placed about 300 feet from the front of the column. We could see in the distance the ghetto's main gates opening for our exit. As we marched slowly through the gates, we had very mixed feelings. We recognized familiar sights we had not seen since our incarceration in the ghetto. Being outside the walled ghetto gave us a small sense of artificial freedom. Glancing at the German guards quickly reminded us of reality.

The column turned onto a narrow road leading to the countryside. No one knew, and the Germans wouldn't tell us, where we were going. Some of us expected to be taken to the railroad station. When we turned and marched in the opposite direction, some of us felt it was a good sign. We found ourselves marching through the openness of the snowy white countryside as the city was left behind. The scene was similar to that in the movie Dr. Zhivago—Siberia, desolate, cold, and forbidden. The German guards, now on motorized vehicles, began to speed up the column. We were ordered to run, then to stop, then to run again, continuously running into each other. We became hot from running and many began shedding the extra clothes they were wearing. Many people fell and could not continue. They were placed in the ditches along the side of the road. We heard shots in the distance and knew what had happened.

I remember a particular incident. One man fell. I was holding on to my dad's hand. The old man fell next to us and the German guard who was alongside forced my dad to carry him on his back and run with him. Dad was running with all that extra weight and I was scared that he might fall and be left

54

behind. The old man died on my father's back, and as the guard moved to a different location in the column, dad was able to put the dead man down.

As people discarded articles to lessen their weight, one dropped a bottle of blue denatured alcohol used in some cooking stoves. Another German SS guard alongside of us picked it up, gave it to my dad, and ordered him to drink it while we were running. I knew it was poison, and if dad drank it he would not make it to where we were headed. He pointed the muzzle of his submachine gun at dad's ribs and shouted "Drink." I began to cry and my mother began to cry also. Dad opened his mouth and began to drink it but he allowed most of the alcohol to run out of the side of his mouth that faced away from the German. I didn't even know what was happening. I thought he drank the denatured alcohol. Later along the way he told us about it.

Several hundred people had dropped out of the death march. We had already traveled several miles and began to wonder if any of us would ever reach our destination, or if another destination even existed. The uncertainty was more than we could bear. We saw nothing in the distance that resembled civilization. Both sides of the road were lined with small country farms and barns. Occasionally we would pass through a young forest. The countryside was not at all familiar to me as we continued deeper into unknown territory.

The SS guards became more brutal, beating us with their rifles, whips, sticks, with anything that could inflict pain. They enjoyed having this supreme power over so many defenseless people. For them, it was like a small boy in a chicken coop scaring all the chickens and not having to account to anyone for his misdeeds. They made us do double time. After eight miles on the road, many were so exhausted, they just gave up, dropped along the road, and awaited execution.

I had already shed most of my clothes and had discarded all the items I took from home. I was perspiring profusely. I was thirsty and grabbed some snow to eat along the road. My feet were getting very tired and I wondered how much longer I would be able to continue. The feeling in my legs had vanished. I felt that any moment I would take my last step and that Dad would have to carry me the rest of the way, if allowed to.

With desperation, I moved to the side of the column so that I could see ahead. To the left of the road, about one mile before us and about two miles to the left of the road, I saw what looked like a large camp. The fence posts and barbed wire silhouetted in sharp contrast against the white cover of thick snow. As our column made a 90° left turn onto the road which led to what looked like a camp, I felt relief. I felt a surge of new energy entering my weakened leg muscles as I anticipated that we might be allowed to rest, once we arrived.

The road was as straight as an arrow, about 30 feet wide. It continued for approximately two miles or so. The road continued on past the main gate, deep into the camp. As we approached the main gate, I observed the shape and size of the facility.

The shape of the camp appeared to be that of a giant square, surrounded by ten-foot fence posts and barbed wire. Guard towers were located at all corners and also spaced evenly along the fences. The towers were equipped with searchlights and manned by Ukrainian guards of an anti-semitic background. The main road split the camp in half. The barbed wire continued on both sides of the road inside the camp with a 50—feet of no—man's—land zone on both sides of the road. I saw barracks evenly spaced, only four— feet tall, with straw sloping roofs on both sides of the camp. As we approached the camp, I saw the main gate and what appeared to be SS guards, with weapons, guarding the gate. The camp commander was also at the gate with his chauffeur and private automobile. The SS guards were accompanied by large German shepherds. That added an additional measure of fear to our already grave situation. To the left of the gate was a small guardhouse and there was smoke coming out of the metal chimney. Electric wires and telephone wires swung from a nearby pole down toward the small structure. Each side of the camp was also divided into many smaller sections, each fenced with barbed wire and guarded gates. I observed very few people moving about. I didn't know if the camp was deserted or if everyone was trying to keep warm in the small barracks.

Both halves of the giant gate opened inward as the head of the column approached. The SS continued driving us even harder, as if this was to be a critical part of the march. Several hundred feet down the road, another gate opened to the left and we were driven in, as cattle into a corral.

I heard harsh German voices shout "Everyone can rest." I fell to the ground, still holding onto my father's hand. My brother was on my right side, while mother was still holding on to my dad's arm. We began eating snow even though we knew that in this overheated condition the freezing snow could be harmful. I felt the snow melting beneath me as I was gasping for breath.

I laid down on the cool snow, face down, and rested. A few minutes later, after I caught my breath and gathered some strength, I pushed myself up by my arms, and lifted my eyes to see if all my relatives had made it. I saw my grandmother, uncles, aunts, and cousins. They were all there. We had arrived in "Kelbasin".

My parents, brother and I all dressed up taking a leisurely Sabbath walk. The sign above my father's head reads "FRYZIER". It translates to "Barber" in English. This photo was taken in front of Dad's barber-shop.

Chapter 5

Kelbasin

It was here in Kelbasin, that my heart was first severed and left me with scars that have remained unhealed to this very day. Although my stay here was no more than just a few weeks, the events that occurred here had a major influence on my development and how I was to view the world and my future role in it.

Kelbasin was the first camp I had seen. Nothing looked familiar. There were no tall buildings: only barracks with low walls and the straw roofs which were no more than four feet off the ground. I couldn't figure how we would stand up in there once inside. The camp was partitioned into many smaller sections with just a few barracks in each one. Each section was surrounded by barbed wire fences with a small guarded gate. It appeared that it was not permitted for the people to intermingle.

We heard voices shouting "On your feet!" I lifted my left hand from the snow and noticed that it had turned light gray. I had no feeling of pain or discomfort. I immediately knew from overhearing past conversations that it could mean frostbite. I knew children my age who had suffered from frostbite in Grodno. I remembered the pain and suffering and eventual amputation of body parts. I hated myself for allowing it to happen to me. I was so tired at the end of the march from our ghetto that I had allowed myself some much needed rest. Rubbing my hand would further damage it since there was no feeling. I unbuttoned my jacket and slid my frozen hand under my right armpit. That was the only warm place I could think of at the time. We got up from our brief rest and formed a column facing the commandant. The officer shouted, "Column face right, and march." We began moving again. A gate opened and we were placed into a section of the camp from where a transport of Jews was loaded into a train and removed the night before. The SS packed as many as one hundred into each barracks—men, women, and children. We were all still together. Our main concern was that all our relatives would be placed in the same section. We stayed close together, and luckily it so happened.

About one hundred people were assigned to each barracks. I can't recall exactly how many of us there were, but I remember that it was very crowded. We opened up the barracks door and this is what we saw.

It was a dugout three feet deep with a dirt floor and exposed dirt walls. A very narrow corridor extended from the front of the barracks to the extreme rear. On both sides of the corridor were wooden bleachers three or four rows high. They looked more like six—foot shelves extending from front to rear on both sides of the corridor. A very small wood—burning stove was located at the center of the corridor, and next to it was a very small table with two stools made of wooden crates. Above the table hung an electric wire that contained a low-wattage electric light bulb at the end. One small obscured glass window was located in the wall opposite the door at ground level. There was some yellow straw scattered on the ground.

We tried to pick the best location, but how were we to choose? Is it best to be near the door, or farther back? Which shelf would be best? The lower shelf was easier access but people would have to climb over you to get to the top. I ran to the center of the barracks, near the light and table. I also felt that by being away from the door we'd be better sheltered from the cold. I did not want to be all the way to the rear in the event we had to vacate in a hurry. These were decisions which had to be made quickly!

My mother, brother, and dad followed me and we chose our spot in the bleachers. The barracks filled rapidly with people escaping the cold, and choosing their place. In a very short time all the available space was filled. It suddenly became warmer inside from the human heat. Snow which was tracked in turned the dirt floor to mud.

Each barracks had to select a "barracks leader" who was to be responsible for all the people inside and for dividing the food rations. He would be the only one in the barracks to have any contact with the SS authorities. We were not allowed to go outside without permission and the light would go out at dark. Everyone had to be counted prior to the light going out and the barracks leader had to report to the

SS.

We were allowed to rest the remainder of the afternoon. We went to sleep on the crowded hard shelves with our clothes on. We cradled close together for warmth and felt uncertainty as to what tomorrow would bring. During the night I experienced overwhelming pain and a tingling sensation in my left hand. I knew that it was a positive sign. At least I had feeling. The color of my hand turned a dark blue. To me, it meant some circulation was present. I had to try moving my hand as much as possible regardless of the pain. I had to restore circulation. By morning, the color of my hand returned almost to normal. I felt that the danger of permanent damage had passed.

We were awakened early, at sun—up, and directed to go outside for a head count. The same procedure occurred at all the other barracks and at the other sections of the camp. We had to stand out in the freezing cold until all the people were accounted for and the authorities were sure that no one was missing. I made a fist with my left hand to shelter my damaged fingers from the cold.

We were allowed to use the public toilets behind our barracks and to do small chores such as fetching water, and, to move about at designated times. Only one water source was available for the entire camp, and that was outside our section. I had to go through several guarded gates before reaching the hand—operated water pump. When I got there with my small pail, I saw a line about a mile long with people waiting to fill their containers. I had no choice but to wait my turn. When I knew several hours later, it was almost dark. I was beginning to that my mother would be very worried about me already by this time.

We could talk to the people that were in the other section through the barbed wire fence and in turn they could communicate with the people through the fence behind them. That was one method of communication we used to search for relatives and friends and to learn what was going on. We found out that all the previous transports from our Grodno Ghetto arrived here. About once a week a train arrived on the railroad spur behind the camp. The train consisted of a coal—burning locomotive attached to approximately 20 box cars. The SS would fill the train with one hundred people per box car. They were given five days rations of bread and blutwurst and told they were being shipped to Germany to work. We also learned that this camp was just a holding place and that all transports previously taken from the Grodno Ghetto passed through here. The news was shocking, to say the least.

We recognized many of our friends and neighbors who were brought to Kelbasin during the process of ghetto evacuation. We learned from those who had been among the first to arrive from Grodno that this camp was originally built to house fifty thousand Russian prisoners whom the SS killed by starvation. The SS wouldn't feed the prisoners at all

63

for a long time, and then would drop some macaroni into the camp from a low-flying plane and watch the hungry Russians kill each other for a little food. It also provided entertainment for the brutal SS.

Food was very meager here. Only a thin-looking soup with a few potato peelings floating around inside and a loaf of moldy bread was brought to each barracks to be shared by eight. That was our total food rations for the day. Dividing it equally was another big problem.

We spent three days and nights in Kelbasin in this horrible existence. We had not yet removed the clothes from our bodies and had no idea when we could. Itching and scratching were common and people were removing lice from each other the best they could. Removing our clothing was impossible without freezing to death.

Kelbasin was a detention camp. It was used by the SS to house Jews who were available for trans-port to the extermination camps, such as Treblinka, Auschwitz, and Maidanek. There were periods with no available trains—that meant a short extension of our lives. I'd like to make it clear that the lack of available trains was not as a result of troop move-ments, but because the trains were needed elsewhere. Hitler considered the "Final Solution" of equal importance to the war effort and it received equal priority. Often the Wehrmacht (the German Regular Army) and the SS generals were struggling for the use of the same trains, each claiming priority.

On the afternoon of the fourth day, we heard

the sound of a distant locomotive and the clatter of old railroad cars. It was the sound of an approaching train. It soon came into view as it approached the camp very slowly, almost at a crawl. I always liked the clank and clatter of trains. Before the war, I often went to the railroad station in Grodno to watch them come and go. It was particularly exciting to me and I wanted to grow up to be a train engineer. I had never been on a train before and the anticipation of the ride was exciting. But this train moved too slowly, almost as if it wasn't going anywhere. It gave me a spooky feeling. Eventually, the train reached the loading platform of this camp and came to a full stop.

I tried to figure out what was happening here, and why. I listened to many conversations and asked some questions. This is what I learned:

An empty train would arrive. The selected people for the transport would be given enough food to last for a few days. "You are going to Germany to work" is what we would be told. The Jews really felt that the worst that could happen was that they would have to work hard in Germany until the war ended. We left our homes against our wishes, but we were still alive. Certainly by cooperating, they would let us live. As for crematoriums and gas chambers, they were still unthinkable at this time.

The main road that extended into the camp was very long. Inside the camp it was fenced off,somewhat as a freeway might be, on both sides of the road. Three-foot ditches lined both sides. I suppose it was to drain off the water from the melting snow in the spring. Sections of the camp lined the road on both sides and each section had a gate that opened into the main road. It was very easy to open one gate and remove the people from that section without disrupting the rest of the camp—sort of like a cattle corral.

Everyone would line up at the barbed wire fence near the road to see the activity in the main road. We heard galloping horses and saw a convoy of about ten wagons loaded with supplies approaching the main gate. These wagons would bring meager rations for the unfortunate ones who were to take the next train out for the five—day trip to death. The empty cattle train was waiting inside the camp for the wagons with the supplies to arrive. We knew that soon a section would be isolated and the occupants would be loaded into the cattle cars. One hundred people per car would be squeezed in. There were five loaves of bread mixed with sawdust (for additional bulk) and a few "blutwurst" sausages to each car. No water or sanitation facilities were provided except for one empty bucket per car when available.

The SS, numerous and carrying loaded submachine guns, lined both sides of the section gate which extended all the way to the waiting train. As the section gate opened, all the people from that area were forced out through the gate between the rows of SS guards and marched toward the train. No escape was possible at this point. Both sides of the train were also guarded, preventing people from escaping between and under the cars. As the column marched parallel to the train, one hundred people were counted and forced into each car. The doors were then shut and nailed. The doors would not be opened again until the train reached its destination.

Each car had two small windows, one on each side of it. The windows were sealed with barbed wired to prevent escape. The locomotive began slowly moving the fully loaded train out of the camp area. The SS, their job accomplished, returned to their quarters. The empty supply wagons were prepared to leave the camp. Security was relaxed as the loading process was over.

One morning, a week or so later after head count, I observed a convoy of horse—drawn wagons driving briskly along the main road outside the camp. The horses were kicking up the soft, powdery snow which had fallen the night before. They turned left onto the road to our camp and were picking up even more speed on the straight road leading toward the main gate. The gates opened wide before the lead wagon approached, making it unnecessary for the horses to slow down. The drivers were waved through by the SS guards as they entered. After all the wagons were inside, both gates quickly closed behind them. It was obvious that a transport was about to leave, but what we didn't know was which section would be selected.

They needed some volunteers to help unload the wagons of bread and blutwurst for the next transport. My father was one who volunteered. My dad approached a Polish wagon driver whom he knew from Grodno, gave him something of value, and made a deal with him to be smuggled out of camp in his wagon. Dad came over to the barracks where we all sat and told us that he was trying to escape in the wagon and would return tomorrow to help us escape also. There wasn't much time for contemplation, and naturally my mother, brother, and I were scared. What if he didn't make it? Would he be able to return to help us? Many questions flashed through our minds with no time left to put our thoughts into words. He had to leave immediately to help with the unloading.

After all the bread and blutwurst was unloaded, there was much confusion. Dad laid down in the bottom of the wagon. The driver threw a blanket over him to cover him up, whipped the horses and they took off like lightning. By this time, all the wagons were unloaded and a column of 12 large wagons pulled by a team of two horses each, manned by Polish drivers wearing white arm bands for identification, began racing down the road leading to the main gate and out of the camp. We saw the main gate open wide for them and in seconds all the wagons were outside the camp walls. The guards just motioned them all through the gate without a search, which was very unusual. The wagons and drivers disappeared into the distance. I continued looking until their silhouette was no longer visible against the snowy white background of the empty fields. My family and I watched from behind the barbed wire fence, which we clenched in our hands, not knowing if we would ever see Dad again. Tears came to my eyes as I watched his wagon disappear in the distance.

I took my mother's hand and we left for the barracks, where our few personal belongings which remained with us after the death march from Grodno were being guarded by my grandmother. We were all very sad and lonely. The thought that Dad might not return to help us was more than we could bear. Mother, grandma, and my brother were crying. It was up to me, I felt, as the oldest man in the family at age ten, to comfort them and assure them that all would be well—because we were such good, religious people, God would not let anything bad happen to us. I felt a heavy load resting on my shoulders but somehow I felt that I could bear that load if I had to. Mother gave me a small pot and asked me to go to the well and get some more drinking water for the family. I took the pot and ran to the well, where the line was half a mile long. I knew that I had to get water and could not return empty handed. Looking at the line, I figured that it would take at least six hours before I could get some. Dad was not around to help me and I had to make a decision. I befriended an elderly man in line near the well. I told him that my mother was sick with fever. I asked him if I could please get in line ahead of him to pump some water for my mother, and I would also do the pumping for him. Inconspicuously he allowed me to get in line in front of him without anyone noticing. I pumped the water, and with a satisfied feeling ran to Mother with my first procurement. Mother praised me for being so resourceful, which in turn gave me more strength and confidence. Night came and we all laid down to sleep on the straw—covered bleachers without undressing. It was cold and we had no blankets. We snuggled close together to keep from freezing in our sleep. The entire family cried privately that night. I held back my tears as long as I could. I finally gave in to my emotion when I thought that everyone was sleeping.

The next morning we were awakened at 5:00 a.m. by some SS soldiers shouting, "Get up and out of the barracks!" We were forced outside into the bitter cold for head count. All the barracks were emptied of people. Everyone, the young, the old, and the sick, had to come outside in front of their barracks to be counted. That lasted for two hours until all barracks counts were completed. This time the count took longer because there was one man short. We were finally allowed to return to the barracks and get relief from the cold.

We were constantly being watched by the tower guards, who were warmly dressed, with their loaded rifles pointed in our direction, just looking for an excuse to fire at us. They watched us from enclosed towers with smoke emitting from the metal chimneys. I despised them having all that warmth and authority over us. There was nothing for us to do. We were waiting for something to happen.

A few more days had passed and uppermost in our thoughts was the fearful fact that it was almost time for the train to return and pick up another transport. What section would be selected next? I kept watching hopelessly through the barbed wire fence for my dad. When would he come for us? Was he still alive? How could he save us? There were no answers for any of these questions. My brother and mother cried all the time. There was never any question in my mind whether my dad would return for us. I knew that he would if he was still alive.

I walked outside into the bitter cold. I couldn't stay in the barracks any longer, even though it was somewhat warmer. I looked into the distance and saw nothing. There was no movement of any sort outside the camp and visibility through the barbed wire fence was very good. I could see for miles down the main road.

Suddenly I heard wagon drivers shouting to their horses and saw galloping horses with wagons approaching from the distance. I was hoping that Dad would be coming back to help us, but chances were slim. As the wagons approached the main gate, the SS guards opened the gate, and as before the wagon drivers didn't even have to slow down to enter the camp. There were seven wagons in this convoy with one driver in each. After all the wagons entered, the gate closed. I noted one driver get off the wagon and head toward us as others unloaded the supplies. It was my dad, and I became overjoyed but didn't make a sound that could give him away. I ran quickly and told my mother and brother of the good news. Dad was dressed in a typical peasant outfit, fur hat and

71

white arm band around his left arm just like a typical Polish peasant wagon driver. Dad hurriedly rushed over to our barracks and said to Mother, "I don't have much time. I'll try to get the children out today and will return soon to get you and your mother."

He somehow got hold of one of the wagon drivers and paid him off, then took his place to drive the wagon to Kelbasin.

Father said to my brother and me, "Quickly follow me to the wagon." Even the short trip to the wagon was not without risk. We had to pass several guarded checkpoints. My dad had a pass, and the right clothing with a proper white arm band on his left arm. He would have no problem returning to the wagon, but what about us? His plan was totally impractical with little probability of succeeding, but it was a chance we had to take. We made it through one checkpoint and ran rapidly toward the next. There was a lot of commotion, people shoving and asking questions. I was close to my dad and my brother was a few feet behind. At the next checkpoint I rushed through holding Dad's hand and my brother was held back for questioning. There was no time to turn back, and dad shouted to me "Come on, we will get him later!" I turned around and saw the disappointed look on my brother's face, with tears in his eyes, watching us silently. That was the last time I saw my brother. I followed Dad's instructions and moved on. At the next checkpoint I was stopped and the guard asked me, "Where are you going?" I replied, "They sent me over there to give a message to the driver," or words to that effect and he let me through.

As we approached the wagon, Dad said to me, "When nobody is looking, get into the wagon fast and lie down." I studied the wagon as I stood beside it. It appeared to be twenty feet tall. The wheels alone were bigger than I was. How will I ever climb inside, I asked myself. In my mind I began making plans how to get into it in the shortest possible time. I decided that the left rear wheel was a good place to start; I was less likely to be seen. I would climb up the wheel spoke and enter the wagon from the rear. My eyes were focused on Dad, waiting for the signal to act. The wagon was unloaded, and as the workers jumped out of the wagon, Dad gave me the signal. I leaped onto the wagon wheel and was inside in less then a moment. Dad watched me do it. Suddenly the German SS turned around, hit the horses with his whip and shouted "Raus!" (move on). The horses let out a loud shriek and took off in a convoy. Dad's wagon was next to last. Dad said to me, "If there are any problems at the gate you will have to jump out." I replied, "okay."

The main road to the gate was packed hard with lots of snow. The wooden wheels with iron tires made for a very bumpy ride. I crawled near the front of the wagon so that I could hear Dad's commands, and he knew that I was right behind him. I had to be hidden from view or it could mean instant death for trying to escape. The convoy was now less then 600 feet from the gate and the horses were galloping at great speed. Dad said to me "The lager master is at the gate. They are searching the wagons, you have to jump out. I had no time to contemplate. In seconds we would be at the gate. If discovered, I knew that I would be shot right there at the gate by the lager master, right before my Dad's eyes. I very quickly crawled to the rear of the wagon and rolled over the rear gate and jumped to the ground. Without losing a single precious moment I rolled off the road into the ditch to avoid detection.

My head, face, and clothes were completely covered with snow. I almost blended into the background. I looked up, raising my eyes only slightly above ground level and saw that I landed near the fence, only fifty feet from the main gate, and all the wagons, including Dad's, were outside the gate already. They were so close, I could almost touch them. Just then the lager master got into his automobile and drove away. I saw my dad get out of the wagon and walk over to the SS guard at the gate. He was talking to him. He gave him some soap and asked him if he would like him to bring some whisky next time. I was so close I could hear the conversation. Dad maneuvered the guard so that his back was toward me, and Dad could see me inside the camp in the ditch watching him. This was a once in a lifetime chance to escape. No command from Dad was necessary. I quickly got up, ran through the gate and jumped into the wagon as Dad was watching. He said goodbye to the guard and we sped away as quickly as the horses could run on the slippery icy road. The gates closed behind us and we were gone. We went back to the Grodno Ghetto. Where else could we go?

Five days later, another convoy of supplies was leaving for Kelbasin. Dad again made arrangements to be a wagon driver. He drove the wagon with supplies to Kelbasin to try to get my mother and my brother. I was left behind in the ghetto. When Dad arrived there, they were all gone, taken on a transport the night before. He returned to the ghetto with the bad news and we cried together all night long. It was the first time in my life that I was separated from my mother and brother for so long. I missed them so much.

"Would I ever see my mother and brother again?" I kept wondering. I didn't even have a chance to kiss them goodbye. I left them so abruptly and so unintentionally just a few days before. I felt guilty. How could I do such a thing to them? They must have been unhappy to be separated from us also. They were forced to board the box cars without us. I am sure that they also felt that in the last moments of their lives, we were absent. Those were my feelings and my thoughts that night.

This photo needs no explanation.

Chapter 6

Back at Grodno Ghetto

My mother, brother, and the rest of my family were separated from us. The thought that would not leave my mind was that we might never see them again. The pain was unbearable to me, for I missed them so much. The hope that someday we would be together again was a major factor in keeping Dad and me going forward each day. That hope was with us throughout the war. I had a strong feeling that someday we would meet and be together again. I had never known anybody who had lost his family—almost the entire family—by the age of ten. My only friend and relative left was my father. If anything at all happened to him what would I do? I was brave, but not brave enough to make it on my own in a hostile world. I hoped and prayed that Father would be well and be with me. Dad and I found ourselves back at the Grodno Ghetto. Where else could we go? The Polish people didn't necessarily like Jews. The few that might have wanted to help were scared for their lives. There was literally nowhere else to go except to our own kind in the ghetto.

But things were now much different. Dad and I were alone. We could not return to our previous apartment, which was in the sealed—off zone. The Germans were looting and taking everything from our homes and shipping it to Germany. We no longer had any personal possessions. The only things that we could call our own were what we wore on our backs at the time of escape. It was awful not being able to return to the home were I was born and had been growing up. Dad and I were assigned a bunk with others in a small crowded apartment. We informed the remaining people in the ghetto of what we went through since we left on our transport and what they might expect in the future. Some believed us and others were skeptical. Only about 25 percent of the original population of 20,000 Jews remained. It was shocking to see so few people left and we knew that soon there would be none.

My dad made contact with a distant cousin of his, Zelik, who had been a baker in the past. He had a bakery before the war and was doing some baking in the ghetto when he could obtain flour. He was in his late fifties, but looked much older than his age, suffered from tuberculosis, and had a chronic cough. We became closer now that we had only each other. We moved to his place for mutual support.

Once a week, a transport of 2,000 people would leave. One month had passed since we escaped from Kelbasin and there were only a few hundred Jews left in the ghetto. So far, we had managed to elude the transports by hiding. We hid in abandoned houses, attics, and cellars. We were running out of places to hide and time was again running out.

We knew that we would be taken with the next transport and there was nothing we could do about it. We had resigned ourselves to the fact that God's will would prevail and we placed ourselves in His hands.

The remaining Jews, including the three of us, were rounded up like cattle and placed in our synagogue for ultimate disposition. That night, someone came up to my Dad and said, "Do you want to escape with us? I know where there is a cellar, stored with provisions, where we can hide." My Dad was very strong and daring and the man wanted him along. Dad informed him that he had an 11-year-old son and an elderly cousin who would have to be included. The man agreed, begrudgingly. He continued, "There are approximately 11 partisans [Freedom Fighters] who will join us in our hideout at a later time." Quietly, Dad informed his cousin and me that the four of us would attempt an escape that night.

It had to be that night. We learned from Kelbasin that you can't put anything off or it might be too late. It was around midnight and there was a lot of chatter in the crowded synagogue. Dad motioned to me and to his cousin to move closer to the window. The four of us sort of blocked the window and Dad tried to unlock it behind him as he faced the front with us. Once it was unlocked, he pushed the window open quietly. Our leader jumped out first, then I jumped and he caught me. The window was eight feet from the ground. Then my dad's cousin was lowered and Dad came last.

Once outside, we had to move fast. We depended on the man to show us the way. I felt if anything happened to him, such as being shot, we would have to return to the synagogue. In other words, our lives were in his hands. There was much snow on the ground and now it was again snowing heavily. The searchlights surrounding the remaining ghetto illuminated the large falling snowflakes like a huge ribbon. We were concerned that our footprints could lead the SS directly to our new hiding place by morning. Quietly we walked through the darkened empty streets, not whispering a sound to each other, as we listened for possible SS guards that might be patrolling. We dodged searchlights as we kept visual contact with each other, staying no more than 10 feet apart. The last man in our single file column wiped our footprints from the snow with a jacket. Luckily for us, it continued snowing all night, so our footprints were completely covered by morning.

About half an hour later, which seemed like an eternity, we arrived safely at our destination. Our guide pushed the door open and we walked into a house, wondering if anyone was inside. It was empty. In the darkness, he guided us into a closet and knocked on the wall gently, and a knock from the inside was returned. We threw a few boxes aside, climbed up into a hidden entrance at the top of the closet, and then descended into a deep hole in the cellar which was to become our hiding place.

Inside the cellar were 12 men with guns who were determined to fight the Nazis in the forest and disrupt their source of supplies. Zelik and I were not warmly welcomed by these partisans. Zelik was too old and sick, and I was too young. They greeted us begrudgingly.

The cellar was a deep hole, a rectangle, about 20 x 30 feet and about 10 feet deep. The walls were bare dirt and so was the floor. It was recently dug, and I have no idea what became of the excavated dirt. At one end of the cellar were two large mattresses; next to them was a small table made from a couple of wooden crates. On top of the table was one lit candle. Oxygen had to be conserved. The candle burned day and night. No outside source of light was available in the cellar. A few smaller wooden boxes served as stools. Against the entire opposite wall were wooden shelves for provisions. On the top shelf were stored about twenty giant loaves of pumpernickel bread. Each loaf was about 24 inches in diameter. The bread had several holes through which mice entered and left at will. There were also some large dried salamis, preciously guarded from the mice. The lower shelf contained a few cooking utensils, dishes, cups, and pots. I observed a few sacks, with holes in them, containing beans and rice. The rodents were entering and leaving the sacks, scattering the contents as I watched, unable to do anything to stop them. They were too many and had burrowed deep into the dirt walls. In one corner were two fifty-gallon metal drums. One contained drinking water and a scoop, and the other was for toilet facilities. A small curtain covered the area where the sanitation drum was located. A few pillows and blankets were scattered on top of the mattresses.

During the daylight hours, Polish workers arrived to remove furniture and anything else of value. We heard them everyday as they worked inside the house. They talked among themselves and we could hear their conversation clearly. We had to remain perfectly quiet during those hours. Any small noise could give us away. Dad's cousin still had a chronic cigarette cough which made us all very nervous. The partisans told my Dad that if he couldn't keep cousin Zelik quiet, they would put him to sleep. One of the men did put a pillow over his mouth when he had to cough.

At night when the Polish working party went home, we would go up briefly for a breath of fresh air and to stretch. We had to be careful not to leave any evidence of our presence. It felt good outside in the open. Looking through the window at the stars, I wondered if I would ever have the opportunity to study astronomy. I enjoyed looking at the sky and wondering how far the stars and planets were from earth. Before the war, on starry nights, Uncle Yudel would teach me about the stars. He pointed out the Big Dipper and other constellations to me. I was fascinated with the vastness of space.

On the third night, the moment of decision approached. The leader of the group said, "We are going to join other partisans and fight the SS in the forest. We will leave tomorrow night." That seemed the most logical choice, since staying here for a long time was impossible.

Everyone wanted to go. My dad was informed that I couldn't go with them because I was only eleven years old, a child, and could endanger the rest of them. Cousin Zelik couldn't join them either because of his age and bad cough. I felt devastated overhearing the leader whisper these words to my dad. I heard Dad reply to him that I was very strong and could keep up with the rest of them and that he would take full responsibility for me. The reply was. "We cannot take that chance." My Dad became angry. I could see the anger in his face as his face turned almost white. I was becoming a burden to him and I knew it. But what could I do? I couldn't just say, "Go without me, I'll be all right." He was stuck with me and it could cost him his life.

In this group of men was a middle-aged jeweler whose name was Mr. Wise. He was too scared to go with the partisans into the forest. My Dad, having no choice,reconciled himself to staying put. His conscience could not permit him to leave me behind after just rescuing me from Kelbasin. If I could have joined my mother and brother at that time I would have done so. I could not bear to see the disappointed look on Dad's face as he was left behind.

All the others left that night, taking with them food, guns, and ammunition. Dad was left in the cellar with an eleven-year-old child, a sick cousin, and a scared jeweler. If any action was to be taken by us, Dad had to be the leader.

We spent several more days and nights in the cellar. We listened to the Polish workers talking during the day. At night, we went up for a breath of fresh air. We never saw daylight. We kept track of the time by the voices of the workers and our watches. We mostly slept during the day and spent our waking hours at night. We didn't want to take the chance of being detected by an accidental sound or cough.

One evening after we descended from our fresh—air break, I overheard Mr. Wise whisper to my Dad, "I have many gold and diamond necklaces, gold watches. and gold coins in my suitcase. Do you know of anybody that would be willing to hide me from the Germans until the end of the war?" Dad replied, "I don't know."

Dad had many Polish friends. One was my grandmother's janitor and caretaker who had been happily employed by my grandmother for more than twenty years. Some were customers from his barbershop. It would have been to our benefit, also, to find a hiding place for the jeweler. It would relieve us of the responsibility.

Dad continued, "If you like, we can leave this hiding place, go to the village nearby where I know some people, and see if we can make arrangements for you." Leaving the ghetto was very risky. If we were detected, we could be shot on sight. The jeweler agreed, and Dad said, "Good, we'll go tomorrow night, just you and me." I said to my father "I want to go too, I don't want to be left here alone with Zelik. I don't want to be separated from you again." My Dad tried to convince me that it would be better and safer for me to remain, and counseled me on the danger and the risk. I told Dad that I knew of the risk and wanted to go anyway. If anything happened to him, being alone in the cellar with Zelik would be as good as being dead.

Dad consented to take me along. Zelik was too scared to remain in the cellar alone so Dad was forced to take him along also, even though his presence would endanger our lives.

We began making preparations for our journey, which was to take place the next night. I packed my little black suitcase with what few belongings I had accumulated, some old clothes, a few frayed towels, two pairs of socks, and a wool cap that I could pull down over my ears. Cousin Zelik gathered his few belongings, Dad took a small bag, and the jeweler packed his little black suitcase with the precious possessions.

Dad explained to us the route that we would take: "We will leave just after dusk. It will take several hours on foot to reach the village. We want to leave early in order to arrive at the village at a decent hour and not have to awaken and frighten our Polish friends. We will leave our hiding place intact. As we leave, we will cover our footprints well and make several circles around other houses to confuse the workers, distracting them from our location. We will walk close together in the total darkness without uttering a sound. We will take the following route. When we arrive at the cemetery we will climb the ten-foot wall, avoiding the searchlights that scan the horizon. We will descend the other side of the wall into the cemetery. We will cross the cemetery in total darkness, being careful not to trip over the gravestones. When we reach the barbed wire fence at the end of the cemetery, where the Polish sector begins, we will slide under the barbed wire and crawl down a small embankment into a running creek. We will try to cross the creek where it is shallow in order not to wet our clothes. When we have crossed the creek, we will be outside the ghetto. We will remove the Star of David patches from our clothes and speak only Polish. We must act inconspicuously as we walk among the Polish people until we reach the village." We had to remember every word he said—even the smallest mistake could be fatal.

The next evening arrived all too soon. W e

dressed with all our warm clothing. My Dad took the ladder and placed it near the escape hatch, and one by one we climbed the ladder to the surface. We extinguished the burning candle and camouflaged the entrance to our hideout well. We looked out the windows and the entire area looked deserted. We saw searchlights scanning the ghetto; it was easy to avoid them. Walking outside the house in total darkness was a frightening experience. There was no moon that night, which was a blessing, but it hindered our visibility. We would have to feel our way, most of the time in total darkness. We walked very quietly. The packed snow made low crackling sounds beneath our feet. I used a piece of cardboard to scatter our footprints. We walked around a bit, hiding our footprints as we felt our way in the pitch dark night.

No one uttered a sound. Cousin Zelik gave a few muffled coughs that made us nervous. Within twenty-five minutes we reached the cemetery wall. The wall was much taller then I had imagined. I could barely see the top against the dark sky. The searchlights were scanning the cemetery and there was no protection from them other then the gravestones. Dad whispered quietly to me. "You go first, I'll give you a push so you will have less to climb." I was scared, but the need to continue overcame my fear and I jumped on my Dad's shoulders and he lifted me as high as he could. I grabbed hold of something and began climbing. When I reached the top, I squatted until the searchlight passed over and then jumped to the ground of the cemetery. When I landed, I fell right into an open grave six feet deep. I felt like an animal being trapped for caging. To make matters worse, I felt something soft beneath my feet. I reached down and it was a dead body not yet buried. My heart almost jumped out of my chest from fright, but I did not utter a sound. One scream and it would be over for all of us. I had an unforeseen problem—to climb out of a six-foot-deep grave. A six-foot climb up a straight dirt wall is not easy for a grown man, but for me, a boy of eleven, it was an almost impossible task. I feared if my Dad and the others couldn't find me, I would be left behind. I thought I would be buried alive the next morning when the Polish workers arrived. I was terrified that a ghost might pull me by my leg. The several minutes in the grave, waiting while the searchlight passed again so it would be safe for the others to climb over, seemed like an eternity. Many thoughts passed through my mind as I stood motionless, braced against the wall, waiting for Dad and the others to cross over. I waited patiently as the others climbed and crossed the fence. I heard Dad call my name quietly. "Hirshel, where are you?" In a crying soft whisper, I replied, "Here, I fell in." He felt his way toward me and we made contact. He laid down on the ground and stretched out his arm, which I found in the darkness, and he pulled me out of the grave. We threw our arms around each other and held tight for a few precious moments. It was time to continue. There were many bodies scattered about from the day before that the Polish detail crews had not yet buried. The ground was frozen several feet deep and digging graves with a pick and shovel was very slow work.

There was no time to spend recovering from my ordeal. We moved quickly and silently, watching for more open graves and unburied bodies. As the searchlights continued to scan, we paused briefly each time they passed.

We crossed the cemetery where the ground sloped sharply toward the creek that we had to cross. We removed our shoes and pants and waded in silence through chest—high ice cold waters, and then scaled the bank to town. I could see well in the darkness, for my senses were sharp, and I was ever watchful for the danger which seemed to be around every turn and behind every shadow.

We removed the yellow Stars of David from our clothing, so as not to be recognizable as Jews (that in itself was punishable by death). Entering the town, we assumed the mask of local citizens, speaking in Polish. We walked in the shadows toward the outskirts of town, where my grandmother's former janitor resided. He, a good Christian, was very nice to us. He felt badly for us. He was definitely against Hitler's policy toward the Jewish people. We felt that if anyone could help us, he would. We rapidly advanced, with our main objective to locate his residence. We had been walking for about an hour and a half when we quietly walked up to his door and knocked gently. It was late at night. All the lights were out in his house. The rest of the houses were dark also. There was no response. We knocked again, this time a little harder. Within a few moments we saw a light come on and someone was coming to the door. The door opened. He stood there in his nightgown, half asleep. When he saw us his face turned white. "What are you doing here?" he said, looking in both directions as if to see if we were followed. My Dad took the initiative in telling him that this man, a jeweler, wanted someone to hide him from the Germans. He would pay well. He had money, a great deal of it. About that time, the janitor's wife, a short, heavy—looking lady in a dark wool bathrobe and a wool scarf around her hair, came to the door. She shouted, "What are you doing here? Do you want to get us shot?" and slammed the door shut in our faces.

We were tired, exhausted from the tension of the escape. Our minds were numb. It was late at night and decision making was impossible due to our fatigue. We couldn't stand there and do nothing. We had to continue.

Dad said to us, "Let's get back to town, to the Polish sector. I know of another person who might help us."

As tired as we were, we had to undertake that five mile walk back to Grodno. There were curfews in force and even Poles weren't permitted to be on the streets late at night. We used back roads and side streets to reach our new destination.

"What if we are turned away here?" I asked my Dad in Polish. "What will happen then?" I knew he had no answers, but I had a question, and I had to ask it. Dad just said, "We'll see."

We reached the second house. It was already two o'clock in the morning. We could barely stand on our feet. We gently knocked on the door of my Dad's friend. A lady looked out from an upstairs window and saw us standing at her door. She put her finger to her mouth instructing us to remain absolutely quiet. She came down the stairs, quietly and slowly opened the door, and asked us what we were doing there. My Dad explained the story about the jeweler who had much money and needed a place to hide.

We wondered if she would be willing to hide him from the Germans. She directed us inside and led us to a small closet under the stairs which led to the second floor of the house. She instructed us to remain perfectly still until she came to us in the morning.

We were unbelievably grateful to her for allowing us inside her home. We needed sleep more than anything. We were thirsty and hungry, but the need for sleep and rest was overwhelming.

The space under her stairs was very small—about 3 x 7 feet with a very low ceiling. There was not enough headroom to sit. We had to remain in a lying position. The floor was dirt. The wooden stairs had about one—quarter inch spaces between the risers. We could see very plainly through the cracks. I had to urinate urgently. Luckily there were some old whisky bottles lying around and I used one of them. Dad's cousin Zelik managed to control his cough, thank God. We laid down close together and went to sleep.

The next morning we heard many footsteps. They were the sound of boots. We heard German being spoken. My heart stopped for a moment and I couldn't breathe. Through the cracks, I saw Gestapo people in brown uniforms going up and down the stairs. My goodness, where are we? Surely we have been betrayed, I thought! I felt that this was my last day on earth! I knew that the time was coming closer for us to be caught, but somehow did not expect it yet. Dad, Zelik, and the jeweler were affected by this latest terror more than I was. I expected somebody to have a heart attack. The jeweler was the one who appeared to be the most frightened.

I heard everyone's heart pounding as we laid there with eyes wide open. I even thought that the Gestapo might hear our hearts pounding from fright. Shortly after, the Gestapo happily thanked the Polish lady for a nice breakfast. As they left the house, our eyes were fixed on them through the cracks between the riser facing the front door. The spit—polished black boots were only inches from our heads as the risers bent slightly under their weight. I could see them clearly—even their facial features were visible.

The Polish lady came over to the crawl space under the stairs and motioned us to come out. She first bolted the front door. The lady asked incredulously, "Do you realize where you are? Upstairs is the Gestapo residence. Had you come during the daytime you would have been shot. The Gestapo forcibly took over the upstairs of my house." Luckily for us, she had no love for Nazis and agreed to help us. We moved about and stretched while she made us breakfast: home—baked bread with butter and jelly. What a treat! She also made us some hot tea. It was the best breakfast I had in more than a year. Because of her association with the Gestapo, she was able to procure food and supplies. She ran a boarding house for the Gestapo. She informed us that she would hide the jeweler in a barn down the road. She continued, "You can leave the jeweler here, and you had better not leave until dark." The problem was that at night the Gestapo returned to her boarding house. She said that would be no problem. "You will wait until the Gestapo go to sleep. I will come and let you out when it is safe. I will provide a safe hiding place for your friend, don't you worry!"

That night, the landlady made a special dinner for the Gestapo. She served them many of their favorite dishes, including some special wine that she had saved for a long time. They partied a good part of the evening and then went to sleep somewhat intoxicated. Shortly afterwards, she came to our hideout and said, "Get ready to leave now." In the darkness of the crawl space, I grabbed the little black suitcase and rushed to the front door, with Dad and his cousin right behind me. We had to move fast and undetected to return to our hiding place in the vacant portion of the ghetto—it was the only safe place we could think of.

We again had to walk clear across town to the creek, cross it, and hike up the embankment to the cemetery fence. We crawled under the barbed wire fence leading to the cemetery and crossed the cemetery in total darkness in order to avoid being spotted by searchlights. We had to watch out for dead bodies and open graves. Then we climbed the ten foot fence back into the nearly deserted ghetto. We made our way through the streets to our former hiding place. Luckily for us, it went somewhat smoother, for we had been there before and it was familiar to us. The tension we felt began to ease as we neared our destination. We had finally arrived safely!

We removed the obstruction from the hidden entrance to the cellar and descended below ground. We lit a candle and found everything intact, just the way we left it, except for one thing. This time there were only the three of us—Dad, Zelik, and me. We were exhausted from the dangerous trip back to our hideout. I undressed and opened my little black suitcase to put on some dry clothes for the night. To my amazement, instead of finding my clothes and personal possessions, my eyes were blinded by the riches of a king's treasury. The suitcase was filled with gold, glittering diamonds, necklaces and earrings. The contents of the suitcase sparkled brilliantly in the dim candlelight. Gold coins in different sizes and various shades of gold, from many countries, spilled over my mattress! Some were yellow gold and others bronze gold. I particularly remembered the U.S. Liberty twenty—dollar gold pieces! American money was familiar to me because my grandmother had once shown me an American gold coin.

This suitcase was much heavier than mine. I had failed to notice the difference in weight in the haste of my departure.

I quickly realized what had happened. I called to Dad and showed him the contents. I had in my possession Mr. Wise's suitcase and he had mine, filled with old clothes and worthless junk. It did not take us long to decide that tomorrow night we must make the dangerous trip back to town again and return Mr. Wise's suitcase to him, even though it meant risking capture and spending another day under the steps of the Gestapo. Dad said to us, "This time I'll go alone, it will be less dangerous and I can move more quickly." I begged him to take me along. I was too scared to be there alone with Zelik. I began to cry. Dad counseled me on the danger involved. I said to my father, "If you are caught, what good is my life here alone? How long can I survive in this cellar without you?" I continued, "If you are caught, I want to be caught also. I don't want to be left alone in the world." Dad agreed that we would take the trip together once more, the three of us.

We spent the rest of the night looking through the contents of the suitcase. I came across a very large Russian gold medal, about three inches in diameter and an eighth of an inch thick, of solid reddish gold. It looked pretty to me and I asked my dad if I could keep it, and he said yes. My dad also took six twenty dollar U.S. gold coins and put three in each of the soles of his shoes. There were so many coins and so much jewelry that what little we took was insignificant. We slept the following day while the Polish workers were in the house above us. We needed to rest for the strenuous journey back to town the following night.

We awoke early the next evening and began getting ready for the trip to town. We no longer heard the workers and we were reasonably sure that darkness had already fallen upon the empty ghetto. Silently we climbed out of our cellar hiding place. The ghetto was empty and we felt safer making the trip the second time. We were more familiar with the terrain and the obstacles now. We went to the gate, over the fence to the cemetery, which brought back the horrors that I had experienced there two nights before. We descended to the river bank, entered the icy cold water under the cover of darkness and crossed the fast flowing stream at the same place as before.

We walked across town to the house where the jeweler by now had discovered the dilemma he was in, and wondered what was to become of his life. We made certain that it was very late at night when we arrived and that all the lights in the house were out. Dad picked up a small pebble and threw it at the window where the lady was supposed to have been sleeping. We hid from view in the event we picked the wrong window. After the landlady opened the window, Dad came out of the shadows and revealed his identity. The woman then came down and opened the door for us. We already knew the direction of the crawl space under the steps and headed right to it. The lady quietly closed the front door and went back to sleep.

In the morning we again heard the Gestapo get up, have breakfast, and talk among themselves. We could see the color of their eyes through the wide spaces between the steps. After they left, the lady of the house again bolted the front door and let us out of our hiding place. We informed her and Mr. Wise how it all happened. Dad explained that I took Mr. Wise's suitcase by mistake and was sorry for all the anxiety we had caused them. Mr. Wise, who had been hiding in a small corner in the attic was brought down to join us. His eyes shined with disbelief when he saw us. He hugged us and cried from joy. We also told them about the few gold articles we had removed from the suitcase. The jeweler replied, "It was certainly all right." We spent the rest of the day eating and talking, waiting for evening to come so we could leave again to return to our hideout in the ghetto.

During our conversation, the lady mentioned to us that a small group of partisans were captured in the forest and that they were all killed by the SS. She overheard the Gestapo talking about it. From the description she gave us, we determined that it was the group from our cellar who refused to take me along because of my young age. Dad, who was also left behind on account of me, felt that, unknowingly, I had saved his life.

Some of the Gestapo stayed up late that night. It was one o'clock in the morning before it was safe for us to leave. Then Dad, Zelik, and I set out again in the heavy darkness of night. There was no moon out that night, and as we walked through town we accidentally bumped into a couple of drunks walking the street late at night. We politely apologized and quickly went on, so as not to get into lengthy conversations with them. We had no lights to help us along the way, so returning to the ghetto this time took much longer. We walked slower and more cautiously.

We saw a slight reflection in the river from the scanning searchlights, so we knew where we were. We followed the river bank to the exact spot where we crossed each time before. After crossing, we walked up the embankment, under the fence, into the cemetery to the ghetto fence. Carefully we climbed the ten foot fence into the ghetto and proceeded to our hiding place, which was just a short distance. It wouldn't be much longer before we would feel the security of our hideout, remove our wet clothes, and get some badly needed rest. Our sanctuary was now in view. The weather was beginning to turn warmer and the snow was turning into slush. There was no need to worry about our footprints now. We reached our house and walked inside. I approached the entrance and noticed that the empty crates in front of the camouflaged entrance were arranged differently than the way I left them when we departed the day before. I didn't pay much attention at first and removed them from the entrance door at the closet. I removed the cover at the hideout entrance and lowered myself down into the cellar. I went first because I was smaller and could go down faster to light a candle for Dad and Zelik to see their descent.

I felt my way around the darkness, feeling for the area on the shelf where I knew the matches were kept. I found them right away and proceeded to light a candle. I extinguished the match as the candlelight began to fill the room. I couldn't believe what I saw!

The entire cellar was ransacked. Everything in sight was destroyed and spilled. The cellar was beyond recognition. There was nothing of value, so nothing was taken, but everything we owned was rendered useless. I became completely speechless. I couldn't utter a sound. I just waited for Dad to come down to see for himself. The sight spoke for itself. All Dad said was "Oh, my God."

It was obvious that our hideout was discovered the day we took Mr. Wise's suitcase back to him. "It probably happened while we were under

97

the staircase closet waiting for nightfall to come." Dad said to us, "Had we been greedy and kept the gold for ourselves, we would have been discovered the day before and probably shot." I replied to Dad, "Yes, that is true, but had you gone alone and left me here for safety, I wouldn't have been here when you returned."

There was no way that we could risk spending another day there. The Polish workers would probably bring some SS officers to show off their discovery. We only had a few hours to make a decision.

I don't know what kept me from breaking down in such a hopeless situation. I just wanted to die; there was nowhere else to go. I didn't want my Dad to know how I felt and cause him great grief. It was the end of the road for us. There were no more Jews left in the ghetto. They had all been shipped to Kelbasin. The entire Grodno ghetto was vacant. Of the 20,000 Jews that were here a year ago, to the best of our knowledge, we were the only ones remaining. My Dad was only 37 years old at that time and he was destined to have to make a decision not only for his life but also for ours. He was confused and did not know what to do. He sat down on the floor and said, "Let's rest awhile." There was silence. No one spoke and we were thinking. About twenty minutes passed and then Dad said, "Lets go to Bialystok. There is a large Jewish community there. We will join them." Bialystok was located about 75 miles southwest of Grodno, not a short distance to make on foot. The danger of being arrested on the road was considerable. Cousin Zelik and I had no ideas. We nodded our heads in agreement. We were too tired to even say yes. Dad said, "Let's get a few hours sleep, but we must be out of here before daybreak." We laid down on the bare dirt floor, cuddled close for warmth, and went to sleep.

A few hours later, I was suddenly shaken by my Dad. "Come on, get up, we must leave now." It was 4:00 a.m. We had to be out of the ghetto by daybreak. We again removed the yellow Star of David from our clothing and quickly vacated our hideout. We left the ghetto and walked along a country road carrying paper bags to make us resemble peasants going to work. We were on the way to Bialystok before daylight.

*These photos of "DACHAU" were given to me by an American Soldier who was one of our **Liberating Angels**.*

Chapter 7

Bialystok

We knew that the 70 mile road to the
Bialystok ghetto, would be long and dangerous on
foot, but what other choice did we have, since we
were the only Jews left? The last remaining Jews we
left behind in the synagogue were long gone on their
way to God knows where. We felt as if we were in a
vacuum. There was no one else to touch or communicate with. Every curve in the road could expose us
to sudden danger, and every passing person was a
potential adversary.

It was the spring of 1942, the weather was
turning warmer which made the road wet and
slushy.Our shoes were worn through with large
holes in the bottom. Traveling on foot was more
difficult then ever. During the winter, I was able to
wrap some rags around my feet to keep them dry and
warm. I had no defense against the cold, icy slush
protruding through the holes in the bottom of my
shoes, attacking my dry socks and feet. There was no
one to complain to. We were all in the same
situation.

We had to make some contingency plans in
the event we'd be stopped for questioning. We agreed
to say that we were traveling to Bialystok to visit my
sick grandmother but our wagon broke down along
the road, and as a result we were trying to make it on
foot.

We carried very few supplies—since we didn't have much to begin with. The one thing that we really needed and didn't have was food. We decided to walk up to a farm house we saw in the distance to see if they would be willing to trade some food for soap. We always carried soap with us. It was a readily tradeable commodity.

We approached the farm house and saw a peasant farmer attending to his cow. We spoke to him in Polish, with a big city accent, telling him of our misfortune in having our wagon break down and about our concern in reaching my grandmother in Bialystok. We mentioned that we had soap and were willing to trade for just enough food to last us until the end of our trip. He agreed, went into his house, and a few minutes later returned with a large loaf of rye bread and a hunk of raw salted bacon in his arms. My Dad gave him the soap, thanked him for his help, and we went on our way. We looked back to make sure that the farmer was not suspicious and was not sending for soldiers to apprehend us. We selected a dry spot along the road and had our meal.

Bacon is something that Jewish people are not supposed to eat. Here we were starving—we had to make it to Bialystok and we needed food. I remembered that in Grodno before the war, my brother was very ill with a heart problem. I recalled the doctor telling my mother that my brother, Sender, must have some nourishment. He suggested ham or bacon. The doctor knew that it was against our religion to eat ham. Mother went to our local rabbi to ask his advice. I remember clearly that the rabbi told my mother, "If it is a matter of life or death, it is all right to eat ham." That was the way I justified eating bacon on the road. I felt it was a matter of life or death.

After we ate and rested, we regained some of our strength and continued on our way. Suddenly I said to my Dad, "We still have the Star of David yellow patches in our pockets which we need to enter the Bialystok ghetto. What if we are searched and it is discovered that we are Jews without our identifying yellow star? It is punishable by death!" Dad replied, "If we attempt to enter the ghetto without the identifying yellow patch our fate would be similar." We pressed on with this new heavy burden of fear in our minds.

The first day we must have walked twenty—five or thirty miles. It was getting dark, and we were growing very tired. We began to look for a place where we could spend the night. We saw some barns along the way and thought it would be nice if we could find a dry one separated from the farm house and unattended. We saw a barn just a few hundred feet off the road with both gates wide open. Dad said to us, "Good, we'll head for that one." We went inside. We saw one milk cow, and there was dry straw on the ground. There was another door at the far corner of the barn, so we chose a spot near there deliberately, in the event we had to make a quick escape. We piled the straw against the wall of the barn and went to sleep.

Morning came all too soon and we were awakened by the crowing of the roosters. We didn't want to stay around too long and be discovered by the farmer. We found an empty pail in the barn. We milked the cow and each had some fresh warm milk. It had been over a year and a half since I had milk. It was pleasant experiencing the familiar taste once again.

We slept with our clothes on, so there was no time wasted getting dressed and we were on the road again before sunrise. We knew that someone would be coming to milk the cow very early in the morning, and we did not want to be there. We had to think about things like that constantly, if we were to stay alive. About an hour or so into our walk, a wagon loaded with hay drove alongside of us, not going very fast, but faster than we were walking. The driver said to us in Polish, "Where are you going?" "To Bialystok," we replied, repeating our made—up story. He said to us, "Climb up and I'll give you a ride. I am going about 16 miles, to the next village to deliver hay." We jumped on his wagon while he continued without even stopping.

We were grateful to him for three important reasons: (1) We could rest again, (2) we covered distance while we rested, and (3) the chance that anyone would question our presence would be remote. The wagon ride was the best couple of hours I spent in a long time. I was still a child and enjoyed a wagon ride, but most of all the fear of being caught was lifted from my small shoulders for this brief and most pleasant time. We arrived at the village and the wagon driver told us that he was going to turn off the road. Dad gave him a little something and we thanked him for his kindness.

Refreshed and somewhat relieved of tension,

we proceeded along the road, hoping to make it to Bialystok which was still more than 30 miles away. We came across a farm lady sitting along the side of the road. She had a table made up of a couple of saw horses and a few broken boards. On the table were several baskets filled with eggs. She was sitting on a small milk stool, waiting for passersby to make a purchase. The eggs were of different colors, off—white to dark brown, dirty and unwashed. Dad walked up to the farm lady and said to her, "Would you like to trade some eggs for this pocket knife? I have no money." The lady looked at the knife, examined the blade, and said, "I will give you no more than a dozen eggs for it." Dad agreed and the exchange was made. Dad gave her the knife and we each put four eggs in our pockets. We went down the road a way, found a spot to sit down, and enjoyed our meal.

We washed the eggshells in a small puddle. Zelik took a safety pin that was used to hold up his pants to puncture two small holes, one at each end of the egg, and he sucked out its contents. I learned from Zelik and did the same to mine.

As we continued walking, a new question came to our mind. We were headed to a ghetto where people yearned to be free. We were already free, so to speak, and were headed to a ghetto. The answer came to my mind quicker than lightning. *We had nowhere else to go!* No one wanted us. Now it was plain to me. I answered my own question.

It was late in the afternoon. We knew that we could not make the Bialystok ghetto today. Getting near the ghetto after dark could be very dangerous. We decided to find another place to sleep and would try to arrive in Bialystok by noon the next day.

We noticed an empty wagon without horses not far off the road. It appeared that it hadn't been moved in a while by the way the wheels had sunk into the mud. The wagon had high sides made of wood which could shelter us from view. It looked like a likely place to spend the night, and we did.

The night was cold and the bottom of the wagon was hard. We used each other's bodies for warmth and softness. We were so exhausted we could have slept on rocks.

We got up the next morning, washed our faces in a nearby puddle, and proceeded to conquer the final stretch of road. We had it all planned. Upon arrival in the city of Bialystok, we would pin our yellow Star of David patches on our clothes. We would be picked up by the authorities. We would tell them that we were from Grodno and had been left behind. This part of the story was true.

About 11:00 a.m., we reached the outskirts of the city. Later in the day when we were within one mile of the ghetto, we pinned on our patches. We were only blocks from the ghetto gate when the Polish authorities picked us up and turned us over to the SS for placement into the ghetto.

We were questioned briefly by the SS. They asked us what we were doing outside the ghetto without a pass. We told them part of the truth, that we were left behind in the Grodno ghetto when the last transport was shipped out. We continued, "We were asleep in the basement when everyone left. When we awakened, the place was empty. We decided to go on foot to the Bialystok ghetto where we had friends." Our identity cards were from the Grodno Ghetto. They eventually believed us and threw us into the ghetto.

We passed through the main gate, similar to the one in Grodno. I thought, we did not have to enter the Bialystok ghetto, no one forced us to enter the gate. We could have gone anywhere, but there was *no place to go*. The borders were sealed, and all the doors closed to us.

Bialystok was still untouched. By that, I mean that the Jews were not yet transported out of there. They were at the stage that we had been in one year before in Grodno. Grodno and vicinity were by now void of all Jews and Bialystok's turn had not yet come.

We felt satisfaction mingling with other Jews whose destiny we shared and we no longer felt alone. The ghetto was crowded and people were busily rushing around trying to make a living for themselves.

Bialystok was a big beautiful city with many tall buildings. The ghetto was large in size and in number. The Jewish population was in good health and unaware of the happenings in Grodno. A great amount of food and clothing was still available and a black market flourished. Over the barbed wire fences, the Jewish people traded services and goods among themselves and also with the Polish population.

The Germans did not yet regulate trading over the fence and the ghetto people were not forbidden from it. By allowing this interaction to occur with the Polish people, it relieved the Germans from providing even a minimum amount of food supplies to the ghetto.

Cousin Zelik found an old aunt of his and he went to be with her. My Dad met a man called Orbach. He was from the Polish City of Lodz. My mother had some cousins in Lodz by the name of Dishkin. The Dishkins were a very prominent family who owned and managed a large kosher salami factory and were well known and respected. Orbach knew our distant relatives and a conversation developed.

Orbach was an intellectual, about my Dad's age, very good with words and ideas but short on implementation. He told us of a place where we could stay with him, and a young lady and her brother who also resided in this small apartment. He told us that he moved in with these young people and was providing for the three of them. He introduced my father and me to this brother and sister and informed them that we were old friends. The young couple was kind to us and we were grateful.

There were now five of us living together—the young lady and her brother, whose names I can not remember; Orbach, our new friend and adviser; and Dad and me. We were sitting around the apartment one evening just talking. Orbach said, "If we had some money, we could buy grain from the bakery and distill alcohol in the young couple's bathtub. We could sell the distilled alcohol for a profit and stock up on supplies for immediate consumption and also for a rainy day." Everyone would need to contribute to this venture in order for it to succeed. The young couple had the apartment. Orbach had the connections. My Dad knew how to make alcohol. I didn't know how I could be of help, but I was young and learned quickly.

I suddenly remembered the large gold Russian medal that I took from Mr. Wise's suitcase. I whispered to my Dad, "Maybe we can trade it for lots of food for everybody." Dad informed Orbach of my gold medal and suggestion. Orbach immediately said that he knew just the right people who would make us the best deal, and of course we would all benefit from this transaction.

The plan to distill alcohol in order for us to buy food on the black market was implemented. We set up a still in the bathroom because that was the only room with running water, and the bathtub could be used to ferment the grain. We built a crude still from what materials were available to us, and worked it twenty-four hours a day. I made myself useful by watching the still all night (not by choice—being the youngest, I had little to say about choosing the shift).

This operation had to be top secret. Had the SS found out about it I'm sure the punishment would have been severe. We couldn't even tell our own people where the liquor came from for fear of being betrayed.

I took off my right shoe, removed a piece of felt that I had inserted earlier to take up space in my shoe and also to hide the gold coin, and came up with the heavy gold medal that must have weighed several ounces. I turned it over to Dad. He gave it to Orbach, who later sold it for enough money to provide six months of food for us.

It seems silly to even mention it, but the first

thing I did with some of the money from the gold medal was to go down to the local bakery and buy some fresh donuts. That was the first time in my life that I had donuts, and were they good! I can still remember the taste. We had almost forgotten that life, as it was here, would not go on forever. Sometime soon, the SS would begin to liquidate the ghetto and again ship out its occupants. We were so busy providing for the next day that we had little time to plan for the future. In reality, there was no future for us and we knew it.

Months later, we met a few men who had been on the march with us from the Grodno Ghetto to Kelbasin and who were supposedly shipped out on a transport to Germany, but actually had been shipped to **Treblinka**. They then escaped from Treblinka, and made it safely to the Bialystok Ghetto. They explained with great detail what really happened to those transports. Nobody could believe what they were told! Here is their story.

They told us that they spent five days and nights locked in cattle cars without water. It was so crowded that people had to sit on top of each other. There were no toilet facilities. The smell was awful. Children were crying and the elderly were dying.

The train was very heavily guarded, and when it arrived in Treblinka the doors were unbolted. The SS selected a few healthy men to help with the extermination process. The ones selected were somewhat more fortunate. This was how they managed to stay alive long enough to escape.

As the train approached the camp, the conductor blew his whistle. That was the signal for the guards to open the gates to allow the train to enter and to alert the SS that a new transport was arriving. A few minutes later when the train came to a halt, it was surrounded by heavily armed SS troops carrying loaded submachine guns pointed at the train. Some of the SS also had guard dogs.

Everyone from the transport was made to jump from the cattle car doors, a height of approximately five feet. Many of the elderly injured themselves in the fall. The people were rushed and beaten and made to run around the gas chamber building. The SS formed a circle around the gas chamber. They stood in one place while they forced the Jewish people—men, women, and children—to continue running. They began to shout, "Remove your clothes" and began to rip clothes off the people to show them that they meant it. When everyone was fully undressed and breathing heavily from exhaustion, the doors to the gas chambers opened and everyone was forced inside. The people were pushed and shoved with bayonets until everyone from the transport was squeezed inside while the dogs barked. The doors shut tightly behind them. The gas was turned on.

They told how they watched in horror, helplessly, as members of their own family went through this ordeal. They told how they watched others they knew being killed. Later they removed the naked, dead bodies from the gas chamber to open pits, to be burned. They told how soap was made from human fat. It was impossible to believe their story. I asked if by chance they saw any members of my family there, my mother, my brother. They couldn't confirm my worst fear. In my heart I knew when, where, and how my mother, my brother, and my entire family were murdered. And by whom. I remember it well. I can never forget!

I wanted to adjust my life to the conditions at the Bialystok ghetto. Listening to the precise description of how my family was probably gassed and burned was like pouring salt on my unhealed wounds. Watching other families still intact, children still playing with their friends, brothers, and sisters, made my pain unbearable.

At night as I lay in bed wondering, many thoughts came to my mind. I began to think how much I missed my only brother who was no longer here. There was never any rivalry between us. He was the younger one and my responsibility was to protect him. I remembered my mother always saying "Don't play too hard, don't let Sender run too fast!" My mother always had something for us to eat. I never realized before how much she did for me and how much she had sacrificed for my brother and for me. I had to scrounge my own food now and keep myself as clean as possible. Among other things, I had to learn to wash clothes and cook simple foods like barley, lentils, and rice. I remembered Mother washing clothes on a scrub board. I never realized that someday I would have to do it for myself. How loving and comfortable it was in our tiny little apartment on a Friday night, after the Sabbath meal, when we'd all gather around the warm stove in the darkness while grandmother sang Yiddish lullabies and folk songs. These precious moments were now lost forever, except in my mind. I laid there and cried in silence, not allowing my father to witness my tears.

It was the middle of summer, 1942. The weather was getting hot. Living conditions had deteriorated since our arrival six months before. Fewer work parties were permitted outside the ghetto. Trading with the Poles over the fence was no longer permitted. Food supplies were scarce. Luckily, we still had some money from the gold medal that I sold, and we were earning some with our alcohol still. The SS began to take a more hostile posture toward the ghetto leadership and we could sense that changes were about to occur.

Drinking water and sanitation were the most critical problem. Water was not always available. The SS could turn it on and off at will. Often we were without water for long periods of time. The sewer system was almost non—existent. Most of the sewer ran on top of the ground along the sidewalk. Aside from the bad odor, typhus and other insect—borne diseases developed. Hospitals and medicine were not available and as a result many people became gravely ill. Many of the elderly and children were dying.

Within a week's time, an announcement was made that a transport of volunteers would be shipped to Germany to work in factories. Anyone interested should sign up. I knew what it meant, but unfortunately there were many who did not. Many volunteered to escape the miseries of the ghetto. The people still could not accept in their minds that the Jews were being exterminated. Their hope and faith in God prevailed over reality.

The first transport of volunteers from

Bialystok left the ghetto. Many left their wives and families in the hope of rejoining them at a later time. It wasn't even a week later when another transport was requested.

Grodno and its vicinity were already cleared of all Jews and the complete evacuation of the Bialystok Ghetto had begun. As the second transport of Jews was selected to leave the ghetto, I saw the resistance of the people trying to avoid the evacuation.

In Bialystok, there was no detention camp nearby, the way Kelbasin was near Grodno. Here, the railroad was close, and when a train of boxcars was available, the SS came into the ghetto and rounded up 1,500 to 2,000 people. Like cattle they were marched a few short blocks to the railroad spur, heavily guarded by SS, bearing loaded automatic weapons.

I had seen it all before and was resigned to the fact that further struggle to survive would be futile. I came to terms with the realization that the end would come soon and that it was unavoidable. My morale was, understandably, extremely low. The will to live had left me. The thought of going on living without my mother and brother suddenly did not appeal to me. I was beginning to look forward to meeting them in heaven.

Another month passed. The hot summer days and the continued shortages of food and water in the ghetto added to the sorrow that already existed. Although several more transports of Jews were taken during that time, I had not yet been selected. Had I been selected, I doubt if I would have resisted. I almost wished that my name would be called just to get it over with.

It wasn't long until my reluctant wish became a reality. I don't remember the exact date when my father and I were selected for the next transport. I had my little bag all packed in a corner of the apartment. All I had left to do was to put on as much clothing as I could wear at one time.

Early one morning, the SS troops arrived on our street, unloaded rapidly from their armored personnel carriers and began rushing into the houses. "Raus, get out quickly," they shouted. We were rushed out into the streets. Most people barely had enough time to get dressed, and many took with them much more than they could carry. Some took things that they called precious but which were utterly useless. The entire street became filled with crying children and sobbing adults. Confused and rushed by the SS, families struggled to prevent separation. For my father and me, it wasn't bad. We held on to each other's hands. I only had him, and he only had me. We had experienced similar situations and were better prepared to cope. We knew that we had to stay together at all costs.

After the SS confirmed that all houses in the selected section were vacated and that no one was left behind, the column began marching toward the railroad station. As I left my street, I looked in both directions, taking a last look at the houses on the block, knowing that I would never see them again.

The column continued at a moderate pace toward the railroad station. This time, there was no shoving and pushing, as during the death march from Grodno to Kelbasin. People were getting tired carrying all their heavy belongings. The SS paid little attention to that. They knew that soon, people would be discarding most of what they had brought. By the time we arrived at the station, we were all breathless and exhausted from the heat, the extra clothing we wore on our bodies and from the march. The SS, marched us up a loading platform while keeping the column tight.

There was an additional company of SS along with Ukrainian armed guards at the train. There was one armed soldier at the beginning of each car, one at the rear, and another on the roof, all with automatic weapons pointed at us.

The railroad cars were cattle cars. At the center of each car was a large heavy sliding door. At the side near the front was a 10 x 24 inch opening near the roof. There was another such opening on the other side of the car near the rear not yet visible to us. The window openings were laced with nailed barbed wire.

We were marched up the loading platform and four SS soldiers were counting and assigning one—hundred people to each car. Many families were separated, crying and begging to be together, but it was to no avail. Luckily for my father and me, we managed to get into the same car. There was pushing with bayonets in order to get all 100 in a car. When the door slammed shut behind us, there was standing room only and people were gasping for air. I was shorter than most people. I felt as though I was surrounded by sky scrapers and would suffocate without even being able to say anything to my Dad.

As soon as the train was loaded, we heard the

workers going around to each car, nailing shut and sealing each sliding door. I began to familiarize myself with my new environment and this is what I saw.

There were no provisions of any kind: No food, no water, no toilet facilities. There were the two small windows I mentioned earlier, one on each side of the car, crisscrossed with rusted barbed wire to prevent escape. We tried to form twenty rows of five people each in order to divide the available space equally. We had barely enough room to sit down. Stretching our legs was impossible. SS guards were everywhere, on all sides of us, between the cars and on the roofs. We were guarded like a gold—bearing train leaving Fort Knox. The command post of two SS cars was at the rear of the train. We heard the sounds of an approaching locomotive and felt the sudden hookup as the entire train began to clatter, each car hitting the one behind it as it was connecting. The train moved backwards for several hundred feet as the locomotive completed the hookups. The train stopped, paused there for a few minutes, and then slowly began to move forward. We heard and felt the clatter as the steel wheels went over the rail joints at predictable intervals. The train rolled almost at a crawl as it made its way through the railroad yards toward a destination yet unknown to us.

I remembered earlier, when I said to my Dad that I didn't want to die yet, stating that I had not even ridden a train. As a young child I was fascinated with trains. Riding a passenger train was one of my longed for wishes! I didn't dream that my first ride would be my last, on a smelly cattle car crowded with a hundred people, behind a nailed—shut door going to a slaughterhouse somewhere in Germany.

Our train began to pick up speed as it left the railroad yards and I could hear the coal—burning locomotive puffing vigorously in the distance. Every once in a while we'd get a blast of black smoke that filled our car with soot and made me sick to my stomach. The temperature was rising, air became scarce, and breathing was more difficult. There were small cracks between the boards of the walls. Those of us that were near the wall were lucky. We could put our lips against the open cracks and inhale some fresh air from outside. We rode all through the night. Sleeping was impossible due to constant stopping, starting, slowing down, picking up speed, and the ever—constant whistle blowing in the distance. There was no room to lie down. Any sleep to be had was in a sitting—up position, wedged between four other people. As daylight approached, those who could peek through the cracks in the wall were looking for familiar landmarks or railroad station names to give us some idea which direction we were headed. By noon, we were exhausted from the heat and very thirsty. As our train stopped at a small railroad station to take on water for the locomotive, I recall many of us were trying to stick our hands out through the small barbed wire window with American dollars, watches, and jewelry, trying to exchange them for a drink of water. Some guards took the money and then brought a canteen of water, others took the money and never returned. Once the water was inside the car, and after a short drink, others would try to grab the water container also. In all this confusion and all that grabbing most of it spilled on the floor. I am sure that in the other cars of our train similar events took place.

It was the third day since our transport departed from Bialystok. One more night of the journey to nowhere had passed and another hot day was about to begin. We were tired and dirty, the men were unshaven, and the smell was already sickening. We had to get out of this railroad car. Being packed like sardines for three days and nights seemed worse than death. The people became irritated and began arguing among themselves, fighting for a little extra space and a breath of fresh air. Some people even began drinking their own urine for lack of water. Older folks began fainting from heat exhaustion and some small children were suffocated from lack of air. We were hungry. Many people had unbearable stomach cramps due to the inability to void in the presence of others. We were getting weaker. The SS were counting on this. They knew from previous experience what condition we would be in at arrival, making the "final solution" an easier task. We were ready for anything. We just wanted to leave the congested railroad car. Even death would be a relief from our suffering. We tried asking the guards our whereabouts; they would only reply "Going to Germany to work." Our train again was slowing down to approach a railroad station. As it neared the station, someone in our car noticed the name. It was a small town whose name I can't recall. It was located in Southeastern Poland, indicating that we were heading southwest to Germany.

"What kept me alive so far, I wondered?" I was one of the smallest people in the car. Maybe that was why I was able to lie on the floor near the sliding door with my mouth in the door crack breathing fresh air. I shared this hidden crack with my Dad, thus providing fresh air for him also. We allowed others to sit on us. They did not know if we were dead or alive. Finally the weight of those sitting on me was overwhelming and I had to get up. The train came to a halt and the locomotive positioned itself to take on more water.

I asked my dad if he could hold me up to the little window so that I might see the activity outside. I hadn't seen the outside in three days and wanted to take a peek. Dad asked permission of the ones near the opening. "Could I hold my little son up to the window opening for a few minutes so that he could see the outside? "Dad asked. They agreed because I was so young and weak. He held me up and I enjoyed looking out to freedom and watching unrestricted activities. After only a few brief minutes of looking out, a big strong man pushed his way over to me and said, "You had enough fresh air, get out of here!" He pushed me down to the floor. He took my place near the window and stood there breathing the fresh air himself. Suddenly I heard a shot. A bullet hit this man in the head and his brains splattered all over the car and some of it hit my face. I almost fainted from shock and got sick to my stomach. The man who was standing by the window fell to the floor, dead. Everyone in the car reacted violently to the shock. Some screamed, others fainted, and everyone else cried with fear. There was no way to remove his body from the car, so his body was pushed over against the wall and used for a seat. There was nothing else that could have been done under the circumstances. This was the first time I saw a man being killed so close to me, so violently, and bloody. I never will forget that! After I recovered from the initial shock, I remembered that I was at that window only moments before. Had he not pushed me aside at that particular time, I would have been the one hit by the bullet. Dad grabbed me in his arms and stared at the fallen man with disbelief. Observing this horrible event made my heart almost stop. My heart began to pound with fright as those thoughts went privately through my mind.

We heard other shots being fired. I could only imagine what was happening to the rest of our transport. The train shook violently and began moving again. We knew that we were not headed for **Treblinka** and that provided some mental relief for the time being. We wanted to believe that the Germans were telling us the truth, that we were heading to Germany to work as they had told us. We were getting the wrong signals. Their treatment toward us and random unprovoked shootings were in conflict with their words. The train picked up speed and our senses gave way to the rhythmic clatter of the steel wheels against the rail joints. We were already too weak to feel pain or hunger. Weakness was the only sensation that was felt. I am sure that others died quietly somewhere in our car. In such crowded conditions it was difficult to tell.

Suddenly, we heard a very loud rifle shot and

a bullet entered our car through the roof at a forty—five degree angle. It passed through the ear of a man who was sitting a row in front of me and slightly to the right. It passed through my left sleeve, barely grazing the skin of my elbow. I felt heat and wetness at my elbow; that was how I knew that something touched me. The bullet then landed in the stomach of the man in the row behind me, slightly to my left. The person with the wounded ear began bleeding profusely and someone wrapped a rag around his head, bandaging his ear. The rag became saturated with blood and a second towel was also wrapped around his head to stop the bleeding. I removed my coat and saw that my wound was slight. It was more like a minor scrape and I was able to stop the bleeding almost immediately. The man behind me with the bullet in his stomach began turning pale and died from internal bleeding shortly after. His body was also pushed over near the wall and used for seating. Had I moved my elbow only one inch more to the left at the time of the shooting my entire arm might have been splintered. "Why was I being spared" I asked myself? "How much longer can my luck last?"

I lost track of time. I believe it was the fifth day on the train when someone looking out through one of the cracks in the wall saw a sign reading "Lublin." We had no way of knowing that we had arrived at our destination—the death camp of **Buchenwald.**

Chapter 8

Transport to Buchenwald

Our ill fated death train with its human cargo, entered the "KZ Lager" (meaning Concentration Camp) Buchenwald, at an ever—slowing pace. Before it came to a complete halt, we heard voices giving orders in German. The train stopped. We heard the stomping of boots as more soldiers took up positions surrounding our train. Then there was silence. A brief moment later, we heard a new command being given in a loud German voice. All the doors opened simultaneously. Capos, (the camp Jewish police) along with the SS troops, began rushing everybody out of the cars. Buchenwald was an "Extermination Camp," (meaning that it contained a Killing and Burning Facility, such as a Crematorium and Gas Chamber).

The SS camp commander, or "Lager Fuhrer" as he was called, selected a privileged number of Jewish men, known as Capos, whom they treated somewhat better, to maintain order in the camp and to also execute their will on the prisoners. The Capos received extra rations and better—fitting clothes.Their appearance and dress were different from the general camp population. For example, if the Nazis wanted two hundred men for a work detail, they would call in the Jewish camp commander and tell him what they wanted and he would get subordinates to come up with the personnel. On the other hand, when they wanted one thousand more people for the gas chamber, the SS Lager Fuhrer summoned the Jewish camp commander and instructed him to come up with a list of that many names. He often had to make the choice of which ones would be cremated the next day. If he could not provide the requested list, he would be removed and someone else would be selected to replace him, and many were willing. Often the camp commander had to pick people he knew and respected—even friends and relatives. I noticed the sadness in his eyes as the number of people to select from became fewer as he proceeded with his horrible job. The SS also provided the Lager Commander and Capos with alcohol. They used it frequently to drown their sorrows.

Most peoples' legs were cramped from sitting in one position for so long, making it difficult to get up. The Capos had to help remove the almost lifeless bodies from the railroad cars. The ultra weak and sick were immediately separated from the others in the transport. The man sitting in front of me who had his ear shot off and was wearing a bloody rag wrapped around his head was also removed. These people were never seen again. Only God knows what became of them. The dead bodies were also removed from the cattle cars and counted. As our column was marched, hurriedly, alongside the train toward camp, I observed several crews working, removing the dead from the train.

Our column left the railroad yards in the direction of Camp **Buchenwald**. It was only a few miles away. It felt good moving our legs again after the five—day train ride. We asked the guards where we were headed and what was going to happen to us. We were told that we were going to Buchenwald. First we'd get a bath and be deloused and disinfected and then sent off to work in a factory. We wanted to believe that but it was too good to be true.

As we arrived at the main gate, both sides of the wooden barbed wire gate opened, allowing the transport to enter. We were then marched over to a section of the camp and found ourselves in a large field surrounded by a ten—foot—high barbed wire electrified fence. It was like a cattle pen. The gates closed behind us and there we were, exposed to the blazing heat of the sun with no shade to protect our dehydrated bodies.

Shortly thereafter, the authorities announced that we would be taken in small groups at a time for bathing and disinfecting. They further stated that all clothes and possessions were to be left behind and that new clothes would be issued after our bath. The only article we were allowed to take with us was our belts. Everything we brought with us, all our most priceless possessions which we carried from our homes onto the train and brought all the way here would be taken from us. My father still had his six twenty dollar U.S. gold coins, three in each of his shoes. Our shoes were also to be left behind. For a moment we forgot that this could be an extermination camp and that the gas chamber could be around the corner, and tomorrow at this time we might be dead. Dad removed the six gold coins from his shoes and picked a fence post, the second one from the corner. He dug a twelve—inch—deep hole with his hands and buried the coins in the ground.

Others were doing similar things with their valuables, if they still had any. We thought that if we survived the war we would return and retrieve our life's savings.

More than half of our transport had already been taken for bathing and disinfecting and it was almost our turn to go. Suddenly a Capo and a German guard came into our midst and shouted, "Are there any tailors here ?" My dad and I quickly replied, "Yes, we are tailors." About fifty or sixty more men admitted to being tailors. The Capo said to us, "Form a column and follow me." The gate to our enclosure opened at his orders and we were taken, placed on wagons and transported to unoccupied barracks. Obviously we were not tailors. Dad was a barber. My grandfather was a tailor and I used to like to sew when I was small. My mother used to let me sew on buttons and even taught me to darn my own socks. My grandmother and Mother sewed often. I used to thread the needles for Grandmother because she couldn't see well. Besides, I would have said anything to get out of there. Taking a "real" bath and being disinfected didn't sound too bad to me. Not when you expect "GAS"

Late that afternoon, after our entire transport was processed and there were no more people left in the holding area, they came for us. We were rushed into wagons and transported to the bath—house. When we arrived, the Capos ordered us to undress and to only take the belt with us. I thought for sure that we were going to the gas—chamber and keeping the belt was only to confuse us and to give us false hope. We had no choice but to obey. We undressed and were led into a large room, with real showers and hot running water. There were even small bars of soap available with the marking "R.J.F." I didn't know what it meant at the time. I found out the meaning later. It stood for "*Rein Yiddish Fett.*" Translated to English, it meant "Pure Jewish Fat." I really enjoyed the shower and drinking as much water as I could. We were long overdue for showers and the availability of drinking water. The water was shut off after a few minutes and two large doors opened on the other side of the shower room. In front of us was a twenty—foot—long corridor that led into another large room. At the doors stood two men, prisoners, with large dusters. They dusted our hair, underarm, and pubic area with DDT powder. We were instructed to go to the next room and the doors closed behind us. The room was filled with piles of clothes—shoes, pants, shirts, and coats. Each one of us was handed a pair of pants, a shirt, coat and a pair of shoes. Nothing fit. I was a child of slight build, but was given pants and coat for a very large man. The shirt I could make do, but the shoes I could swim in. I was the youngest person in that group and obviously there was no children's clothing available.

We had to rush to get dressed and were then marched outside the camp gate to the railroad station where there was a train filled with Jews from Galitzia (a province in central Poland), people speaking Yiddish with a notably different accent, heading for Blyzin. There was one empty car at the end of the train, which we quickly filled. The door behind us was closed and nailed shut.

I really didn't know what had become of all the

people who arrived with us on the train from Bialystok. I can only guess. Buchenwald was an extermination camp. I never saw or heard from any of them again. It was like the earth opened up and swallowed the entire transport of our people all at once.

Barely thirty six hours had passed since we arrived in Buchenwald, after that horrible five—day train ride. Again we were locked in a railroad car for future transport. I couldn't believe it! The locomotive whistle blew three times, disrupting my thoughts, and the train left the station. This time, the car was not as crowded as before. We still didn't know how long we would be on the train. The locomotive began blowing black smoke as the train picked up speed. We settled down on the floor and decided to get some badly needed rest while we could. The thought of the fate of our friends left behind in Buchenwald wouldn't leave my mind. The next morning we felt the train slowing down and could read the station sign: "Blyzin." Nothing unusual happened during the unloading. There were the SS, and many Capos aiding the SS in the unloading of the transport.

Blyzin had a mixture of Jews from many parts of Poland. I heard Yiddish dialects that were new to me. We were led to a barracks which was to be our new home. The barracks was already crowded so everyone had to squeeze closer together to make room for the new arrivals.

One of the first things I did in Blyzin was to trade my newly issued pants for a loaf of bread. When I left Buchenwald, where all our clothes and possessions were taken away, I could keep only my belt. My suit was way too large for me, but of very good wool material. It was in new condition. Here the Polish peasants came near the fence and were willing to trade food for articles of clothing or anything valuable. One of the peasants shouted to me through the fence, asking if I wanted to trade my pants for a loaf of bread. I replied to him, "If I trade my pants for bread, what will I wear?" The Polish farmer replied, "I will throw you my old pants. You put them on and wrap your pants around a large stone and throw them over to me." I wasn't about to throw my pants first. Had they become hung up on the barbed wire fence, or had the farmer not kept his word, I would have wound up without any pants. I hadn't eaten in several days. A whole loaf of bread to share with my dad sounded very good to me. I saw the farmer take off his pants. He wrapped them around a four inch stone. He then wrapped a piece of rope around it and knotted it securely. He threw it over the double fence and miraculously it did not land on or between the barbed wire. I quickly unwrapped it. I removed my good woolen oversized pants and did the same to them. I returned to him the same stone and tied it with his rope. My dad threw them over the fence and the farmer caught them. He took out a loaf of round pumpernickel bread, about twelve inches in diameter and threw it toward us. It landed within our reach. The bread was soft, and freshly baked. Dad and I found a quiet corner and devoured it immediately. It was the only meal we had in a long time and I will never forget how good it tasted. Minutes later the entire loaf of bread was gone, and so were the new pants.

I was already thirteen and a half years old as I began adjusting to my life (if you want to call it that) in Concentration Camps. I felt the Nazi grip getting ever tighter around my throat and I was unable to release my frustrations without risking death.

At Blyzin, the women were kept apart from the men in an adjoining camp separated by a barbed wire fence. Many lined up at the fence to look for relatives and to talk to friends and try to find out what had happened to their relatives. It was a very emotional time. I felt my own loss as I watched and listened.

I don't know how I let it happen. For the first time since I was separated from my mother and brother at Kelbasin, I lost control of myself. We had just returned from a work detail with our shovels. We were all tired and dirty, sweaty from the manual labor over the past several hours. We were dehydrated from the blazing heat. We were in the middle of crossing a little wooden bridge that spanned a small creek with flowing water. The water below was more temptation than I could stand. I dropped my shovel and dove into the creek not thinking how deep the water was. The coolness of the water was invigorating and I drank my fill. I continued to swim under water. I don't remember why I did this. Maybe it was a subconscious desire to escape. The color of the water was dirty brown. I opened my eyes under water and couldn't see anything in front of my eyes. Not knowing how far down I was from the surface I tried to swim deeper. In moments my chest and stomach was scraping bottom. I felt a burning cut on the right side of my chest. The pain was great and I immediately went for the surface. I saw a large amount of red blood around me in the water as my head broke the surface. I felt my chest and there I saw an open cut about four inches long with blood rushing from it. There was still a piece of glass in my wound from the broken bottle that cut me. I removed the glass and put a piece of clothing against it to stop the bleeding. I rushed to my dad for help. He found someone who let him have a scarf and he wrapped it around me to hold my skin together. We couldn't report it to the authorities for fear of being shot. We held the skin together with a scarf until, miraculously, with Gods help of course, it healed, without infection. I still have the scar to remind me of that day.

Three months passed quickly. I was later allowed to do less strenuous labor. My work consisted mainly of operating a button—hole machine, sewing button—holes in Nazi uniforms. I had a large quota to complete each day. It was very demanding. In addition, Dad and I cut hair in the evening so we could acquire a few extra provisions, to help us stay alive.

The chill of autumn was in the air and the falling leaves reminded me of autumn in Grodno. It was always such a colorful time of the year. We were aware that the cold season was just ahead, and wondered whether we could survive another winter.

A sudden order was given by the SS Commandant for all prisoners to assemble at the parade grounds at once. The barracks leaders gathered their people and marched them to the main parade ground, where everyone was again counted more than once. We stood there at attention, for several hours, then we sat on the ground for a while and then at attention again. The Lager Commander arrived in his chauffeur-driven vehicle and addressed the entire camp in German. He stated that the previous night a prisoner escaped and was caught, and that no one ever had or ever would escape from this camp and live. In minutes the SS brought the escaped prisoner before the entire population of the camp. They forced him to kneel before us and shot him in the back of the head with a rifle. His head exploded and he fell to the ground. His body was then hanged from a gallows as a warning to others. We were allowed to return to our jobs with the message clearly imprinted in our minds.

My dad had befriended many of the Jewish leaders. He became acquainted with them while cutting their hair and giving them shaves. Being in their good graces resulted in some extra food from time to time, which was a major benefit. One day, the Jewish Lager Leader passed on some confidential information to my father. He told my Dad that, according to a reliable source, the SS would soon be gathering all the young children from Blyzin and sending them to schools in Germany. He suggested to my dad that he let me go so that I might benefit from the education and remain alive. When dad related it to me, I again resisted leaving him for the same reasons that I didn't want to be left in the cellar hideout in the Grodno ghetto. Dad reluctantly agreed to let me have my way and did not force me to go. On the contrary, when the SS came to round up the children, dad hid me under a blanket in a corner of the shop until the transport of children departed.

Several months later, word filtered down through the underground lines of communication that the transport of children was taken to Auschwitz for extermination. I became the youngest person in Blyzin.

Winter was upon us again. It reopened the wound of the previous winter in Kelbasin where I last saw my mother, brother, and the rest of the family. I never saw them board those cattle cars for the gas chambers and crematoriums of Treblinka. Deep inside my soul, I had hope that I would be reunited with them again at the end of the war.

I adopted a philosophy that would help me cope and survive. I imprinted it deep in my mind and recalled it at will when in desperation: It's true that living conditions are at their worst and we have little to eat, but if we are resourceful and do what the Nazis want us to, we will survive until the war ends.

There were many tailors in Blyzin and a shortage of barbers. The shortage was acute because of lack of sanitation. Many epidemics occurred and barbers were needed to remove most of the hair from the prisoners' bodies. We were originally sent here from Buchenwald as tailors, but Dad and I were reassigned as barbers and as a result, our living conditions improved slightly. Dad was a barber in Grodno and I knew my way around a barber shop. By existing standards, we were treated like doctors during an epidemic. We were given a bit more rations and some extra clothes. My work was hard. My job was to remove the hair from the heads, underarm, and pubic areas with a hand—operated manual clipper. I did it from morning till night, resting my hand every so often. After a while, I just couldn't compress the clipper's spring any more. My dad helped me make my quota when I got too far behind. The bodies of the prisoners were lice infested and every one had lice by the thousands. As my clipper sheared through the hair, it also cut through the lice, dulling my clipper and making it juicy with the blood from the parasites.

Many people, including myself, put our clothes outside our barracks at night for the frost to kill the lice imbedded in them. Needless to say, diarrhea, tuberculosis, and typhoid fever prevailed and thousands died. I recall when I contracted typhoid fever and was very sick with a temperature of 105°. I almost died from the fever. My dad was able to obtain a bottle of soda pop, which I think saved my life. After I drank the liquid, my fever broke and I got better. It is really difficult to say for certain what helped me, whether it was my youth, the determination to survive the war, or the bottle of soda pop. Perhaps it was the combination of all three.

During my illness, I would hide in the barracks underneath some old clothes very quietly while everyone else went to work. After the barracks were vacated, the SS man would enter the barracks to look for the old and sick. One morning, I was feeling much better but still weak. I hid under the stack of clothes and rags as I had several times before. When I thought it was safe, I crawled out from underneath to see if all was clear, and there before me was the mean SS man with a long bull whip in his hand. He commanded me to come out, and when I did he made me remove my shirt, put me behind a wall, and proceeded to whip me. My father was outside being counted with the rest of the men when he heard my screams. He ran into the barracks, informed the SS man that I was his sick son, and begged to be beaten instead of me, for I was too sick to take the punishment. The result was that we were both brutally beaten, but our lives were spared because we were barbers and were useful for the time being.

Shortly after that beating, I developed a large boil under my left armpit as a result of my typhus infection. My father found a Jewish doctor who was also a prisoner. He had no instruments or anesthetic, but he agreed to operate on me with the only instrument available—a used razor blade. His fee for the surgery was a quarter pound of butter. The doctor operated on me in the filthy barracks. He made a two-inch incision under my armpit, scraped the wound with an old spoon, and then inserted a rag into the opening for drainage of the pus. No stitches were used. He wrapped the wound with an old shirt sleeve around my neck for support. The pain was unbearable but I didn't make a sound. I cried quietly. The next morning when I awakened, the entire bandage, even the wrapping around my neck, was saturated with pus. Every few days, the doctor inserted a new rag in the opening. Eventually the opening became smaller and smaller until it healed completely. I never could figure out what prevented an infection. After I recovered, I spent nine more months in this concentration camp cutting hair and cleaning barracks until my usefulness here was exhausted and we were shipped by train to a new concentration camp not yet too well known at that time—the extermination KZ Lager named "**Auschwitz.**"

*These photos of "DACHAU" were given to me by an American Soldier who was one of our **Liberating Angels**.*

Chapter 9

Auschwitz: Gas Chamber and Crematorium

As had happened many times before, several barracks, including mine, were isolated. We were informed by the Capos at the head count one morning, "Everybody is being shipped out immediately to a new camp with better working facilities. Your rations will be distributed soon. You will get a much—needed bath so that you will make a good impression upon arrival at your new destination."

Shortly thereafter, a horse—drawn wagon entered our camp. It was driven to the area where we were assembled. The driver distributed moldy loaves of bread, one loaf for each eight people. We ourselves had to divide each loaf into eight equal pieces. One person in each group was selected to make a little scale. It was made out of a ten—inch twig with two short strings, one on each end of the twig. A third string was fastened to the center of the twig for balance. At each end of the twig, one string was attached. A match stick with sharp points was fastened to each end of the string. After the bread was cut into eight seemingly equal portions, it was then weighed to assure that no one received a greater portion than someone else. It was weighed by puncturing the crust of each portion of bread with the sharp point of the match stick. One man balanced the scale by holding it up with two attached portions while seven others watched intensely to insure equality!

I had no way of knowing how long we might be traveling without food or water, so I put my share of the bread ration into my pants pocket to be eaten later when my hunger pains would be the greatest.

We were not given a chance to return to our barracks to collect the few personal possessions we had. We were told that everything we needed would be provided at our destination.

We were taken to a real bath house, with showers. We were told to undress and a small bar of soap was given to each of us. It was too good to be true. We had hot showers, and towels were also available for us. We were led out a different door and new clothes were handed to us as we were hurried along to the outside of the building. The clothes issued were, again, much too large for me. I had to roll up the cuffs of the pants and the sleeves of my jacket several turns.

The Lager Commander blew a whistle and everyone lined up in formation and began marching toward the waiting train, as directed. My father was at my side; I hoped that the new camp would be better. We boarded the box cars and when everyone was inside, all the doors slammed shut once again. We sat at the track for an hour and a half. The SS and Capos returned to their other duties. A platoon of SS armed guards remained with the train. We heard the coal-fired locomotive approaching and felt the jolt when it connected with the train. We moved in a backward direction for a while. The train came to a complete halt. Some switching was performed and we began to roll in a forward direction.

The transport to **Auschwitz** was as follows:

We were again placed in cattle cars, one hundred people to each car. It was summer and the heat was unbearable. Again, there was no water or sanitation. There was barely enough room on the floor to sit. It was impossible to stretch our legs or go to sleep.

Sitting on the floor, dozing to the rhythmic motion of the train, I began to daydream a little. I recalled the times in Grodno when I wanted to ride a train before I died. Now I felt that I had too many miserable train rides already, yet I was destined to have many more. I lost track of time. I think it was on the third day that our transport went through the railroad station of Krakow and it began to slow its speed shortly thereafter. I felt as if the train would slow to a halt in seconds, but instead it kept moving at an unbearably monotonous pace. I looked outside through the cracks and all I could see were fields. The train finally stopped, switched directions, and again continued at a crawl. This went on for an hour or more. We did not know what was going on. (I know now that it was switching into position to enter Auschwitz.)

Through the crack in the door, I saw a barbed wire fence and I shouted "We have arrived," not yet knowing where. All the people in the railroad car rose to their feet and began looking through the cracks to see where we were. There was shoving and pushing going on for the best position to look out. Soon thereafter, the train came to a complete halt. We heard German—speaking voices through the closed door. Many more soldiers arrived on the scene. They were giving orders in German, which I did not yet understand. When everyone outside was in position, the SS Commander gave the order to open all doors. The doors opened simultaneously and we heard shouting "Raus alle," the German phrase for "Out, everyone." We began jumping out the door, approximately three feet to the ground. Many of us fell as we jumped. Our legs were weak from sitting so long. We could barely stand. The transport was completely unloaded in just a few minutes. We were assembled in a column along the railroad track and again counted. We were always being counted.

I smelled an unusual odor in the air—it was the smell of human bones, I was later told. It smelled something like a dentist drilling your tooth with a high speed drill. You can sometimes smell the odor of the tooth particles vaporizing. I saw an unusually large number of heavily armed SS troops, as well as many men dressed in well—tailored blue and white striped suits and hats. I later learned that they were the trustees whom the SS used for the extermination process. They were the elite Capos. The nickname "Canada" was given to them by prisoners. Canada was symbolic of the good life, and was equated to them. They wore arm bands around their left arm and appeared to be very well fed.

My dad and I recognized one of the trustees and yelled his name, "Yankel? Where are we? What is happening?" He replied to us in a very low, sad voice, so as not to be noticed by the SS guards as we were being shoved into formation by the bayonet-bearing SS troops, "I am sorry to see you here!" He pointed to his right, with his arm arched in a 45° angle toward the sky! "Do you see these smoking chimneys? This is the crematorium. You are all going to be killed today in the gas chamber. I am very sorry that I have to be the one to tell you this."

The terror that struck me was like a large mountain suddenly landing on my shoulders. I became speechless from the realization that I only had minutes to live. I raised my eyes toward the smoking chimneys and had to believe what I saw. The smoke was heavy and fire was visible erupting with the smoke. There was absolutely no chance to escape. I felt only helplessness and disbelief.

This was the closest I had ever been to death. It was right here before me. Up until this point, I never believed that people were being murdered in cold blood for no reason at all, although I had seen many signs to the contrary. I assessed our pitiful situation. We were alongside a railroad track. The empty train had already departed on its way to bring a new transport. We were completely surrounded by the SS troops with fixed bayonets at the unloading dock. *We were inside Auschwitz.* To the best of my knowledge, no one ever escaped from there alive. A special track was built just to deliver the trainload of condemned Jews to Auschwitz. All around us was an electrified barbed wire fence with guard towers located every two hundred feet or so. About thirty feet beyond the barbed wire fence was a second barbed wire fence with SS guards and German shepherds patrolling the space between both fences. Approximately forty feet inside the first fence was a single strung barbed wire. This was the death zone. Anyone crossing that wire was inviting fire from the guards at the towers. I turned and said to my dad, "Dad, is this it? We can never get out of here alive. We will soon be with Mother and Brother." My dad replied silently with tears in his eyes. Most people with us became hysterical, some cried, others screamed, and some jumped toward the electrified barbed wire fence and electrocuted themselves rather than go to the gas chamber.

The SS began shouting and shoving with the bayonets to regain control of the column. We were constantly confronted with new orders to keep us off balance. People were falling and being trampled by the constantly moving masses. More guards arrived on the scene and we were all held at attention while a head count was taken again to verify the previous count.

A new order was levied upon us, "Column turn left and march forward." Our column, with the help of Canada, obeyed the command and began marching like sheep to the slaughter in the direction of the Crematorium. One always had the feeling that sheep on the way to be slaughtered knew where they were going. I am sure that the SS knew that we were aware of the situation and the ultimate fate that was awaiting us.

My position in the column was in the middle of a five per row column, near the tail end. I happened to be in the last car. There were two sickly old men to the right of me. My father was at my immediate left, holding my hand, and there was one more person to the left of him. We had already advanced several hundred feet in the direction of the tall brick smoking chimneys of the crematoriums. The SS guards on both sides of us were marching so close to each other that they almost poked one another with their bayonets. I could see the first rows of our column turning right toward the opened gates of the crematorium. I was wondering how many minutes would elapse before my row would make that deadly right turn. I was literally counting the minutes and seconds remaining in my life. I was no more than fifty feet from the curve. I tried to see ahead and through the gates. Inside the gate, I could plainly see for some distance. The road inside was straight for several hundred feet. The crematorium and gas chamber building, now clearly visible, was made of red brick, and architecturally pleasant to the eye. I saw prisoners with striped uniforms walking around and doing some sort of detail jobs. Some were pushing wheel barrows and others were pushing wagons. I heard music being played by a chamber orchestra. As I neared the gate, I could see the musicians, in striped prison uniforms, seated over to the side playing Beethoven and Bach. My row had already made the deadly right turn and had advanced to only steps away from the entrance. Suddenly I felt something hard around my neck pulling me. I was holding on to my dad's hand with all my remaining strength, and both of us were yanked out of the column as we were about to enter through the gate.

Just as I turned my head to see what had happened, I saw a high—ranking German officer standing on higher ground near the gates and very close to the column. He was accompanied by two junior officers standing alongside. They were immaculately dressed with many medals on their chests and spit—polished black boots worn with riding pants. The one in the middle appeared to be the highest ranking. He was in his early sixties with grey hair showing around his officer's hat. He was heavily built, about 275 lbs. On either side of him stood the junior officers, much younger, both carrying coiled bull whips in their gloved hands and nine millimeter Lugers strapped to their belts. In his hand, the senior officer held a large cane with a curved U—shaped handle. I did not see him grab the cane at the bottom and swing it out toward the column, placing it around my neck and yanking me out of the column. As I turned my head toward him, his hand was around the lowest part of his cane and the curved part was still around my neck. He did not mind that my dad came along and his attention turned toward the walking column looking for others to select from among the prisoners. Before I realized what had happened, the entire column was inside the gates and the gates were closed. By morning, there would be no trace left of those who just entered through those gates of Hell. There were only about twenty of us who were temporarily saved out of the entire column of several thousand, and we did not know why. We were the lucky ones for the time being; they would later use us to do an unthinkable task. The SS guarding us fell into formation and returned to their quarters, awaiting the next transport that would arrive all too soon.

It soon became clear to us that we were saved because we appeared healthier than most and were needed to work in the crematorium as replacements for those who could no longer work because of deteriorating health. We were later forcefully put to work to handle the clothing that was left behind by those innocent victims. The next morning we were awakened just before sun—up for head count. As I rushed outside, my eyes were drawn past the first rays of the rising sun toward the two chimneys of the crematorium where white smoke propelled by glowing red flames protruded from the tops of the stacks. Was it my transport going up in smoke? Was this *"The last Sunrise"* that I was watching? "It can't be, it can't be," I said to myself. The block commander shouted, "Fall in formation for head count." My attention was diverted to the right side of my formation to form a straight line.

Following is a brief description of the events that took place at the Auschwitz Crematorium as I observed them some 47 years ago. This is my best recollection.

All transports arrived by train. After unloading, all the Jews were marched through the crematorium gates, and the gates were closed. Several hundred people at a time were packed into a large room with signs all over stating "Bath House", or "This Way to Bath." Everyone was forced to undress rapidly. A few minutes later, another door opened and everyone was shoved inside. Simulated shower heads were installed in the ceiling to further deceive us. The condemned people were packed in until the door would hardly close. The doors shut tight and poisonous gas was injected into the gas chamber. Minutes later, another door opened at the opposite side of the room and the dead bodies were removed for burning later. While the first group was being gassed, a second group would be undressing. It was like an assembly line. It became my job, along with others, to remove all the clothing from the room rapidly, so as not to delay use of the room. The clothing was removed to a large warehouse, where later it was sorted and searched for valuables. The bodies were searched in the most intimate places; rings and gold teeth were also removed. The ovens were going at full capacity twenty—four hours a day, but still a backlog of bodies was accumulating. Outside the crematorium was a very large ditch filled with human fat. I was told that the Nazis used it for making soap. I saw large pits filled with bodies. I don't know whether the pits were used for storage or for burying purposes to take care of what the ovens couldn't handle. All these things which I saw were unbelievable to me. My mind just couldn't comprehend it all. I saw so much so fast that it all seemed unreal—like a bad dream. After a ten—hour shift of hard labor, we returned to our barracks.

My selected group of twenty joined another small group of new arrivals. We were taken to an area called "Birkenau." It was a section of Auschwitz. A tattoo number was inscribed on our left forearm and we were told that from now on we would be called by number only. We were taken to a real bath house, and after a delousing procedure we were issued blue and white striped uniforms and a striped cap which we had to wear at all times. Afterwards, we were marched to a clean barracks which was to become my home for the next eleven months. This barracks was vacated by a previous group of prisoners

146

who had outlived their usefulness and were put to death. The barracks was cleaned by others, not leaving a trace of the previous occupants. The barracks contained two tiers of bleachers and each one of us was assigned a space.

We were being worked sixteen hours a day—ten hours at the crematorium and the remaining six policing and cleaning our barracks. When anyone got hurt or became sick, he was removed from the ranks and never seen again. As one might imagine, there was an abundant supply of stronger replacements available. Exhausted, we would fall asleep with our clothes on, on the hard wooden bleachers used for beds. Many times in the middle of the night, the SS came into our barracks shouting, "Everyone outside for head count." The head count lasted hours before we were allowed to go back to sleep. By the time this was all over, it was morning again. At 5:00 a.m. we were awakened, and another head count was taken before going to work. We were kept so busy that we couldn't think of either the past or the future. The only thing that mattered was the present. We tried to stay alive one day at a time, knowing in our hearts that our days were numbered.

I recall one afternoon when a head count was taken. All the men in our camp stood at attention for several hours in the hot burning sun out in front of the barracks. There was a large water fountain in the center of our camp filled with clean drinking water. Anyone that could no longer bear the heat and ran toward the fountain was shot en route. As a result, we wouldn't chance it.

Standing at attention for so long in the hot sun was a form of mass punishment for one reason or another. I saw many collapse in the ranks. These were quickly removed to the gas chamber and crematorium. I suppose this was a technique for getting rid of the weak. I stood motionless. The movement of a limb or of your head would certainly invite physical punishment to the offender. As I stood perfectly still, the only movement was in my brain. I was facing the crematorium chimneys and the hot sun was directly above my head, cooking my body. I tried to keep my mind working, hoping that doing so would prevent me from falling unconscious to the ground. There was enough smoke and fire coming out of the chimneys to keep anyone's mind fully occupied. The flames ceaselessly erupted, providing an always—present reminder of what this place was all about.

Every morning when I got up for head count, I looked at the sun rising. Each time I felt that I was watching the last sunrise. I lived each day as if it were my last. Unwillingly, I would turn my head toward the flaming chimneys of the crematorium, and say to myself, "Thank you, God, for giving me this extra day to live." Every day I lived became a special gift from God. I knew that if my turn came to go, it wouldn't be until that evening. I felt almost certain that I would not die today. I was not too certain about tomorrow, for it was in the evening when the sick and the wounded were weeded out.

As the months passed, we grew weaker and thinner from lack of nutrition. Every morning we would find a few dead among us who died quietly in their sleep. Sometimes when it was the one sleeping next to me, I did not become aware of the situation until morning. It wasn't a great shock any more; it was a frequent occurrence, and we became accustomed to it. Many of the very weak and frail whose turn in the gas chamber had not yet come just gave up hope. Some died in their sleep, while others grabbed the electrified barbed wire fence and were electrocuted. It wasn't unusual to wake up in the morning and see charred bodies still holding on to the barbed wire fence. The electricity would be shut off while the dead were removed by our own working crews.

Birkenau was a clean facility as far as camps go. We had much time to police the grounds and to clean the barracks. Our friends from Grodno who were called "Canada," and previously gave us the bad news at the train unloading zone upon arrival, had connections and were somehow able to procure more food. Every time they procured something extra to eat, they would offer me some. I was still the youngest in the camp, and many men sort of adopted me as their imaginary little son.

I don't know how I lasted one year in Auschwitz, living from day to day without any real hope in sight. The ovens were still going at full capacity but the Russians were advancing, unbeknown to us. The SS were preparing to abandon Auschwitz. The gas chambers and ovens had to be shut down when orders came from SS Headquarters to ship the remaining prisoners to Germany. We were given a double portion of bread to last us several days en route. Instead of an eighth of a loaf we received a quarter of a loaf. Most people ate it right away, but I put mine in my pocket to eat later.

We were rushed from our barracks to the bathhouse, and after a real bath we were issued new striped prison uniforms before boarding the train. In all that haste I left my portion of bread in my other pants. The next day, when I could no longer bear the hunger pains, I informed my father what happened to my rations. He became so angry at me that I thought he was going to kill me. He called me names that I would rather forget, but in the end he shared his bread rations with me. I have never forgiven myself for making such a serious error. Dad's decision to share this ration could have been the crucial nourishment that saved my life on the forthcoming train ride. Where would they ship us to now? Where to?

Chapter 10

Night Of Fire At Berlin Railroad Station

I had just reached my fourteenth birthday. Another empty cattle train eased itself through the gates of Auschwitz to the very same landing spur where we had first arrived about a year before. The doors of the dirty, old cattle train slid open, as it had many times before. Each car was packed to capacity with prisoners. After the transport was completely loaded without incident, the doors slid shut, locked and sealed as if they were carrying precious cargo. These sealed doors would not be reopened under any circumstances until we arrived at our destination. We were already too weak, both mentally and physically, to care. We knew from experience that an existence worse than death was awaiting us for the next several days. We were to be without food, water, or sanitation facilities. Not one of us knew where we were going or why.

The train traveled very slowly for several hours as if the locomotive couldn't get up enough steam for the heavy load it was pulling. It might have even been going up a grade. We were gasping for air in the heated car and didn't care about our ultimate destination. We felt that this time none of us would be alive when the doors to our cars would finally slide open. The locomotive quit pulling and we felt the train slowing again. It came to a halt at a remote side track waiting for more important trains to pass, trains filled with wounded German soldiers returning from the Russian front and monition trains heading north to resupply the German army.

It was late in the afternoon. The temperature in the locked cattle car was very high. The two small windows did not provide enough air for the occupants to breathe. We had been sitting there motionless for six hours. At least when we were in motion, the cooler air from outside would seep in through the cracks and we would get some relief. We felt that dying would be a blessing for us, ending our suffering. I felt that I was going to die soon anyway and postponing the inevitable would be much more painful in the long run.

Just as our death wish was about to come true, the train began moving again and the temperature began to fall. It was early evening. It was cooling off outside and cooler air entering through the crack was of great benefit. We traveled all through the night and a second day. On the third night, our train eased itself slowly into a very large railroad station. We heard many trains coming and going as our train proceeded to a side spur. I saw the platform and a sign with the station name through the crack in the door. The lit sign read "BERLIN." We all became very excited when we realized that we were inside Germany. The train came to a halt. Each one of us came up with his own version of why we were there. The train continued moving very slowly, switching tracks for almost half an hour until it finally came to a halt at the most remote track of the Berlin railroad station, where we would probably spend the night for one reason or another. We felt a jerk as the locomotive disconnected and abandoned us on the side track.

It wasn't long after we stopped that we heard explosions in the night, and through the cracks in the door I saw many fires erupting all around the railroad station. German soldiers were running around in confusion and firemen attempted to put out the fires. Explosions erupted more frequently and many trains were on fire all around us. Through the cracks we saw wounded German soldiers, some of them on fire. Monition trains were exploding all around us, adding to the chaos. The train next to us was on fire. We could feel the additional heat from the burning train next to us, through the walls of our box car. The German guards left the scene and abandoned us in the locked box cars. I knew that soon our train would be hit and would ignite like all the other trains around us. The bombs continued hitting their mark, causing one explosion right after another. Steel and wooden objects were flying through the air, igniting other trains, and puncturing cars as they landed. We didn't care so much about dying at the hands of the Allies, but we didn't want to die in the gas chamber. Within fifteen minutes, which seemed like an eternity, the bombing had stopped and everything around us was burning. Shells were still exploding from the burning munitions trains. The danger had not yet passed for us. We could still be hit by exploding shells or catch on fire from the burning train on the adjoining track. By some miracle, our train was spared from the bombs and did not ignite from the surrounding fires.

We realized that the railroad station was being bombed by the Allies. (We learned later that the

British bombed by night while the Americans bombed by day.) At first we were frightened and aware that we were locked in a train which could ignite at any moment. This was not the way we would have chosen to die. I felt that since death was just around the corner, I would rather die by allied bombs than at the hands of the Germans.

The next morning, our locomotive was sent to remove some of the burned cars to clear the main track. It took two more days to repair the damaged tracks. Our black, smoke—puffing locomotive returned to us at the end of the second day and hooked on to our train with a big jolt. We began moving again and a few hours later we arrived at a new railroad station. The sign said "**Oraninburg.**"

It was raining as we unloaded the train. We had to march two miles to our new camp. We could barely walk. The short distance we had to walk seemed like an eternity. We collected raindrops in our folded hands for drinking and the wetness that covered our bodies was refreshing. Some of us who could no longer walk were left in the box cars and the rest of us proceeded to the main gates of the "Katzet Lager" (KZ).

As we passed through the main gates, we found ourselves inside a fenced camp with modern barracks, well—paved streets and sidewalks. It looked like a well-organized army base. There was a lot of activity on the streets. Army trucks rushed by us on the rain—drenched street, spraying us as they drove by. We were led in a column down the main street. The weaker people fell behind and were disposed of later, just like the ones who couldn't leave the train station.

The SS guards wore rainproof pants, ponchos, and boots and were in good physical condition. They looked superhuman to us. Maybe it was because we felt so weak and inferior at that time. We were all led into what looked like a large empty hangar with only straw on the floor. About two thousand of us were packed into this one large hangar which was to be our home.

Each prisoner selected a small spot on the thin straw to make his home. My father told me to stay where I was. He was going to gather some more straw for us to sleep on. A few minutes later I saw a Nazi guard kicking and beating someone on the ground about fifty or so feet from where I was sitting. I did not move from my designated space for fear that my dad might never find me. He had been gone a long time and I was beginning to worry that he might not return. A while later, Dad returned. I told him what I saw; he did not comment.

We were put to work almost immediately doing garbage detail and cleaning up the streets. Once a day we'd get our moldy bread rations and a bowl of thin, tasteless soup that looked more like dirty dish water than soup. This became our routine. A few days later, after work, as we were sitting on the straw in the hangar, my dad took off his shirt. I noticed black and blue marks all over his upper body. I asked him, "Where did you get the marks?" He told me that it was he who had been beaten up a few days before while looking for extra straw in the dim light of evening. A strange feeling came over me. I thought to myself, I saw my own dad being beaten and didn't even know it. I felt very bad and scared. My dad was my hero—being beaten and not being able to defend himself was mentally destructive to what little hope and confidence was still left in my being.

Head count was at 5:00 a.m. every morning. We had less than six minutes to get dressed and out the door. We had to sleep with our clothes on because of the cold and also because it took too long to get dressed in the morning. Some of our work also consisted of digging ditches and carrying bricks or sacks of sand or cement on our backs. Every time the sirens sounded because of the Allies' air raids (twice a day), we'd be rushed to our hangar. After the all-clear siren was sounded, we'd go back to what we had been doing.

We heard many airplanes taking off and landing and I felt that we were near an air base. At night, in the hangar, during the air raids, I kept listening to the sound of the Allied bombers approaching. It was predictable. Almost every night, we heard sirens and then the faint sounds of approaching aircraft. I was one of the first to hear the sound of the heavy, loaded bombers because I was the youngest and my ears were probably better than most. I wished that I could go outside and wave and shout, "drop your bombs here so we might have a chance to escape." But of course our doors were shut and locked for the night. As the airplane engines became faint in the distance, the all clear sirens sounded once more. We knew that the sirens would not remain silent for very long because Berlin was only about thirty miles away and we knew as well as the Germans that Berlin was the squadrons' destination, where the bombs were to be released. The Allied planes would return over our camp again on the way back to England, empty of bombs. The sound of the unloaded B—29 bomber was different, of higher pitch. We could tell by the sound of the engines that the bomb load was dropped successfully. I don't recall any German fighters going up to challenge the Allied bombers, even though we were right on top of a Messerschmitt aircraft factory.

This became a daily routine. It got so that I could tell in an instant which direction the planes were headed by the sound of the engines. I often thought, what if the pilots couldn't drop all of their bombs on Berlin and decided to drop the remaining load on the hangars that were our home? It looked so much like an airplane hangar. We would be destroyed instantly.

I heard a few anti—aircraft batterys open fire at the overhead Allied squadron and I don't recall them ever scoring a hit. After the daytime air raids when we were allowed outside and looked at the sky, I could see the black rings of smoke high in the sky created by the anti-aircraft shells exploding. This went on for three weeks. Every day the routine was the same. The bombers would come, drop the bombs over Berlin, and return empty to England.

One particular Sunday, things were different. Allied planes approached Oraninburg as usual, and as usual the sirens sounded and anti—aircraft fire was sent up. The all—clear siren sounded a few minutes later and we knew from past experience that within one hour the sirens would sound again as the empty planes returned on their way back to England after the bombing run on Berlin. This time when the empty planes approached overhead, the engines sounded different. The sound was low, as under a heavy load. Their engines had the characteristic of high rpm, laboring, hard working, under a heavy load. I told my father that something was different this time. Suddenly, to our total surprise, the B—29s began dropping their bomb load at a corner of our camp—to be more precise, on a young pine forest recently planted. Beneath the ground was a modern, well-camouflaged Messerschmitt plane factory. Bombs exploded nearby and there was total chaos among the Germans. The airplane factory was destroyed, including all the Messerschmitt planes below. The airfield was also destroyed in the same raid. Within minutes, there was total and complete destruction of the entire facility. We found pleasure in knowing that the Allies knew where the airplane factory was located—not at the obvious hangars where the prisoners slept, but beneath the ground under a pine forest. None of the hangar barracks was even slightly damaged; not a single prisoner was hurt. After that, there was no more reason for us to remain here, so we were shipped out on yet another train.

Chapter 11

Sachsenhausen

Homeless and weakened by German oppression, our bodies and minds reflected the heavy toll of four years of inhumane captivity. The end of the war or freedom was nowhere in sight. We had been on the road so to speak, being shuttled to ghettos and to concentration camps, one after another. We had forgotten where home really was, or where we belonged. Living for more than four years with only personal possessions on our bodies and nothing to hold on to created the illusion of being lost in space. The fear of death was no longer threatening. We weren't really living. Death was no longer a negative consequence. We accepted the fact that at death, at least, our souls would be at peace, and being in Heaven with God and with our loved ones was all the pleasantness we could hope for.

We had no idea how the war was going. Isolated from all news sources, our eyes and ears were both blind and deaf to the world around us. We heard rumors, but nothing was official. We had some idea that German casualties were heavy on the Russian front, but there were no signs of shortages of SS guarding our camps.

Again we were rounded up and told to gather our belongings, that we were about to be shipped out. "Where to now?" our souls cried! We marched the two miles to the railroad station, where the transport train was waiting. The train had the look and smell of death. To my astonishment, it was the very same train that brought us here not so long ago.

"Where to this time?" I cried. That phrase wouldn't leave my mind. "Why can't they leave us alone?" I asked my dad, knowing that he had no answers. Most of us lacked the strength to climb the three feet onto the freight car. Our bodies looked like skeletons with bones showing through all over. All the ribs were clearly visible; our stomachs looked concave. Without exception, we all resembled skeletons covered with skin. The muscles in our arms and legs were degenerated to a point where they were no longer visible. Just standing consumed all our available strength. Most of us were suffering from dysentery, tuberculosis, typhoid fever and other chronic diseases.

I don't know how we managed to board the train in the shape we were in. There must have been an unseen power that gave us a helpful push in this critical moment.

The SS guards relaxed their alertness. They carried their rifles recklessly over their shoulders. There was no need for them to show concern. It was evident we were in no condition to escape. They even showed some patience with the slowness of our boarding. They knew that at this point, shoving and pushing with bayonets would show no results. This time they even permitted us to help each other board the train.

This train was less crowded than in the past. There were fewer of us and, as a result, we each had more room. The doors locked shut behind us. We heard a loud locomotive whistle and we were on our way again. The next day our train arrived in Sachsenhausen, only a short distance from Oraninburg. The crematoriums and gas chambers in places like Auschwitz and Treblinka were already dismantled. I felt that at this point we were a burden to them and they didn't quite know how to dispose of us.

We unloaded in **Sachsenhausen** but didn't stay there long, either. I do not recall anything about that camp. I suppose that nothing significant happened there to make an imprint on my mind for later recall. The next thing I remember was leaving Sachsenhausen by train for yet another location.

The year was 1944 and the autumn chill filled the air as a hard winter was advancing. We were about to take another train ride. This was to be our last. Sometime during the middle of the night, we were awakened, and ordered outside for another head count. We were told that we were about to depart from here to a more permanent camp with much better facilities. "The train will arrive shortly," we were told by the Lager Commander. "The food will be more plentiful at the new destination." We wanted to believe it and we did. Nothing, but nothing, could be worse than where we had been up until now. We were just a breath away from eternity and for many in our transport, so it was.

The empty train with open doors eased into position at a loading platform that was the same height level as the open doors. It would be much easier to load the train this time. We were handed an extra portion of bread rations for the trip as we entered the box cars. All the doors were slid shut, bolted, and sealed. I heard the locomotive sound three whistles and someone in German shouted "Take it away."

Our train was heading southwest as we penetrated deeper into Germany. It became more certain that we would never return to our home-town in Poland. Even if we survived the war and returned, there would be no one there to greet us. Through the cracks, we could see the German countryside. It was very beautiful. I saw people walk-ing and dogs roaming around the village streets. I was wishing that I could walk free and breathe the fresh country air that was available to everyone but us. "How many more years can this war last?" I asked my dad. "Won't it ever end?" There was no reply.

The end of the war was still more than a year away. Had we known then how much longer it would last, we would have ended it right then and there. It was the uncertainty of things that gave us some hope.

Our ill—fated, slow—moving old train was heading in a southerly direction deeper into Germa-ny. We passed through the most beautiful, quaint villages, with narrow country roads lined with beautiful tall green trees and old houses, lovingly cared for. Each community had its own church, usually painted white, with the tall steeple reaching high above the homes surrounding it. The move-ment of the residents reflected a slow, peaceful way of life.

It was unbelievable to us, the victims, that such atrocities could go on in such a peaceful land.

The train began to slow down. The houses were spaced much closer together. We must be approaching a city. Everyone was watching through the cracks in the walls for some sort of sign describing our present location. Suddenly someone in our car shouted, "Frankfurt!" It didn't mean much to me because I didn't know where Frankfurt was, but others who were older and more knowledgeable than I, recognized the name and knew our location.

Our train slowly passed through the railroad station without stopping and came to a halt on a side track to take on water and wood. Coal was already in short supply. The German guards got off the train to relax and to buy some provisions such as cigarettes and food. About fifteen minutes later, we heard three whistles from the locomotive, indicating that we were about ready to leave. The German guards returned and boarded the train, and again we were on our way.

The further south we headed, the more beautiful the countryside became. The land was slightly rolling, giving additional dimension to the landscape. You could almost put a frame around each scene and capture its beauty. For a moment, I was able to wipe the pain and suffering from my mind. Like a tranquilizer, the beauty of the landscape dulled my senses and I felt no pain. Several hours had passed. I tried thinking pleasant thoughts to occupy my mind, to make me forget the present reality. Someone shouted, "Stuttgart!" We were in the middle of Germany. "Oh my God, what is going to happen to us now? What are we doing here?" There was much speculation but no one really knew. Our train didn't even stop here. We continued for a few more miles down the road and then stopped for water for the locomotive. Later that night, the train stopped and the locomotive was disconnected. We were left motionless on a side track. The guards were reduced to a minimum number and we spent the night quietly locked up in the box cars.

Early the next morning we were awakened by the jolt of the locomotive hooking up to the train. We continued heading south. Our train took us through one of the exquisite sites in Germany. We had entered the province of Bavaria, and by evening we had arrived at the outskirts of München (Munich). Our transport passed through the Munich railroad station at moderate speed without slowing down much. All the switches were opened and closed in order to accommodate our train, as though we had priority. In minutes, we were out of the railroad station, the locomotive puffing black smoke as it picked up speed. Three nights and two days passed since we boarded this slow—moving death train, when we pulled into the distant concentration camp called Dachau.

Chapter 12

Dachau

The last word in the previous chapter was "**Dachau.**" As I write this word, a sudden chill goes up my spine and engulfs my body. Not just because there was a gas chamber and crematorium there, but because it seemed that there would never be an end to the many gas chambers and crematoriums that the Nazis had built and that I was exposed to. It seemed unlikely that our luck would last forever, and I became convinced more than ever before that sooner or later I would be gassed and burned.

At times, one gets a feeling that something bad is going to happen and it does. That was the feeling that overcame me when our train arrived here from Sachsenhausen. Now, only one month later, the same fearful feeling had returned, this time with much greater intensity. To the best of our knowledge at that time, Dachau contained the last functional gas chamber and crematorium. Why else would they bring us here if not to *burn* ?

There were always many SS guards around us, all carrying submachine guns when the trains unloaded. Looking into all those loaded barrels created a feeling of certain death within me. I deliberately ventured very close to the SS loaded submachine guns. I wanted to take a detailed look at the working parts so that, in the event an SS ever dropped one and I had the opportunity to use it, I would know how. Often when a prisoner was too slow or would not understand a command, he would be shot on the spot. The SS who did it was not accountable to anyone for his horrible act. I wondered why the SS had guns, and were able to shoot at will, and I was worth less than a bullet just because I was Jewish.

The SS were spaced about twenty feet apart, and our column, five abreast, began moving slowly forward. We were marched into the main camp of Dachau. The KZ was in the shape of a large square; the ground was perfectly level and was covered with decomposed granite, very clean. There were the usual three feet of barbed wire electrified fences. A secondary fence, about four feet beyond the first, was also about three feet tall—it was barbed wired but not electrified. The guard towers were erected between the first and second fence, spaced quite close together. The tower guards would walk between both fences to get to and from the tower posts. Inside the camp, about twelve feet before the electrified fence, was a perimeter marked by one single strand of wire one foot off the ground. Between that wire and the first fence was no—man's land. As I mentioned earlier, anyone crossing that wire fell immediate prey to the tower guards, who enjoyed taking shots, aiming for the heads.

I remember my dad warning me not to go near that wire, but it wasn't really necessary. I was fully aware of the danger after spending several years in KZs already. Many people were shot in that zone, some who had crossed accidentally and others deliberately, lacking the strength and will to cope.

Right inside the gate was a large white building with a pitched red tile roof. That was the SS guard house and kitchen. No prisoner was allowed near there unless it was to work in the kitchen, which was special. Working in the kitchen meant extra food, such as potato peelings and other things the SS normally discarded.

A big parade ground fronted the SS headquarters building, and several hundred feet into the camp were two rows of large wooden barracks on both sides of the parade ground. There must have been at least ten barracks on each side. At the end of the left row and to the left, there was a gently flowing river. Across the river bridge was a very nice—looking red brick building with a steeply sloping roof, resembling a chateau, surrounded by large pine trees, nicely landscaped and looking like a beautiful mansion. That was the gas chamber and crematorium. We were later told that anyone who was taken across that bridge seldom returned.

We were rushed to a barracks and were counted at the door as we entered. When the exact head count was reached for this barracks, they stopped admitting and the column continued to the next one. This procedure often separated relatives. There were a few lucky ones like me who still had a close relative near them. I don't recall exactly how many people were squeezed into our barracks, but it was crowded. I tried to select the upper shelf for my bed, far away from the door. It was a bit safer, less noticeable by the constant, threatening patrolling of the SS.

Dachau was a non—working camp, so most of

our time was spent scrubbing the barracks floors and policing the grounds. When there was nothing better to do, we would have head counts that lasted for hours. During these head counts, the entire camp participated. All the prisoners assembled in front of their barracks. First the head count was taken by the barracks master, who himself was a prisoner, and then it was done by the SS to verify his count, then the Jewish camp commander and SS commander counted together for further verification. We all had to stand at attention in formation until the entire camp was counted. If the count did not coincide with the expected number, then a recount was ordered which lasted for several hours more. The sick and dead were also counted.

The temperature continued to drop and winter was almost upon us. The barracks contained only one wood—burning stove in the middle of the center aisle. Even if we had enough wood, the stove wasn't big enough to keep the place warm. Getting enough firewood was impossible. We kept from freezing by clinging close together. How I managed to survive in that camp is still a mystery in my mind. I am not describing our meals because there wasn't much to describe. We were fed a minimum to keep us just barely alive. It was evident by the lack of flesh around our bones that our rations were never intended to keep us healthy.

Among the new arrivals, was a man named Berl Lom. Berl was a man about my father's age, maybe slightly older. He was a shrewd and successful business man in Bialystok. He was great with words but his body was old and weak. He was in a deteriorated physical condition. On the contrary, Dad and I could still move around well on our own. He hoped to benefit by being in our company and in return he offered much advice. He was in business before the war and was quite knowledgeable. He was a pleasant sort of person and we all got along well. One evening we each received our bread rations and divided the loaf of bread among eight. We all ate our bread rations immediately, but Berl Lom saved most of his for later. He was a chain smoker and would often trade some of his rations for a cigarette butt. He usually slept on one side of me and my dad slept on the other side, keeping me between them for warmth and protection.

One morning when we awakened, Berl said to me "Hirshel, you stole my bread ration in the middle of the night while I was sleeping and you ate it." I replied, "I did not steal your bread, I know nothing about it." He continued accusing me. "Somebody cut off the inside of my pocket while I was sleeping, with the bread ration in it. You were the only one who had access to a razor and, besides, you were sleeping right next to me. It had to be you." I began to cry and told my father that I was being falsely accused. "I didn't do it," I insisted. The circumstantial evidence pointed toward me. Both Berl and my father were sure that I was lying, but they did not want to make a big issue over it. They just branded me a liar. I knew in my heart that I didn't do it, but I couldn't convince them of the truth no matter how hard I tried. The false accusation weighed heavily on my shoulders, in addition to all the other problems I had to cope with at that time. No one can ever understand the emotional strain on a person of being falsely accused and not being able to prove his innocence unless one experiences this mental torture himself.

Months later, a group was selected to be transferred to Lager #11 near Landsberg. There was some construction work going on, building concrete bunkers. The selected group, in which my dad, Berl and I were included, was to begin a march on foot to a location some twenty miles away. One morning very early, with no prior warning or preparation, right after head count, our column was ordered to face left and begin marching toward the main gate. Luckily, my dad and I were in the same column, as a result we were not separated.

The march was like one of the death marches you must have heard about. When a company of well fed, warmly dressed SS soldiers on motorcycles and personnel carriers took a group of undernourished, poorly dressed, and tired prisoners for a twenty mile march in the middle of winter, you know that not too many would make it alive. The SS did know that.

At the rear of the column were two personnel carriers whose drivers followed behind and picked up the tired and the fallen. When the vehicles became full, the trucks pulled off into the countryside, and the German guards shot the prisoners in the head and left them in the field for later burial. The trucks would then catch up with the column and start all over again.

Somehow deep inside me was that strong drive to go on, not to give up, not to fall behind. I felt that if I could last just a little longer, the war would end and I might make it yet. I also recalled that I felt that way when the Russians advanced at the Eastern front and I was evacuated from Auschwitz. It was hopeless then, also. I felt that if I fell back, my dad would also slow down for me and his life would be endangered. I would have felt responsible; I could not let this happen. My feet were hurting beyond belief and every additional step became a major effort. I took a deep breath and convinced myself anew that I had no choice but to go on and make it to our next camp, "Lager #11."

It was almost dusk when what remained of our original column arrived within sight of Lager #11. The camp was located in the middle of a dense forest. It was a large clearing surrounded by the usual barbed wire fencing. The guard quarters and mess hall were located outside the main gate. A pit in the ground near the road served as a garbage dump for the kitchen. Inside the camp (we saw this through the barbed wire) were what appeared to be under-ground shacks with straw roofs. Actually it was a 16 x70 foot hole approximately 3 feet deep in the ground with pitched straw roofs overhead. We were led through the gates into our underground barracks. Those of us who remained from the original column collapsed from exhaustion on the wooden shelves (our beds). I again selected a space in the middle of the barracks near the little stove for warmth, for my dad and me. In the middle of the night, we were awakened and given a bowl of warm, watery soup with a few pieces of potato peeling floating around inside. We desperately needed something warm to eat and I consumed it to the last drop. At that point, I didn't know which I needed more, the sleep or the soup. After my meal, I fell into a deep sleep.

At 5:00 a.m. we were again awakened for head count and then work details were formed. We received our daily rations, consisting of a bowl of soup and an eighth of a loaf of bread. After our meal, we marched through the main gate to go to our job site, which was some eight miles away. My job consisted of unloading a trainload of 50 pound sacks of cement. I had to carry them on my back to the job site which was approximately a half mile away, open the sacks, and empty their contents into a cement mixer. Others added water and poured the mixed concrete into wheelbarrows. The heavily loaded wheelbarrows were pushed over to the erected forms and poured. Because of the weakened condition of the prisoners, it took two men per wheelbarrow, one at each handle, to do the job. If any concrete was spilled along the path, the prisoners could expect a severe beating. Our work detail had the responsibility of keeping the cement mixers going. For eight hours or so each day I had to carry those 50 pound sacks on my back from the railroad cars to the cement mixer.

At the end of each day, when the eight hours of carrying cement were over, there was still the eight miles hike back to camp. After a few weeks of that, I was sorry that I hadn't been taken to the gas chamber with my mother and brother at the very beginning of the atrocities. I knew in my heart that physically, I couldn't endure this pace of work much longer. Each night on the return trip to camp, my sweat combined with the accumulated cement powder in my hair and on my body, and hardened. In a few weeks, I looked like I was wearing a cement helmet. I finally had to break it up into small pieces and cut my hair at the roots in order to get rid of the concrete. My lungs also become irritated from coughing up the cement powder that I was breathing all day long.

Dad became a barber and his job, in addition to cutting hair, was to keep the barracks clean while everyone was away on work detail. You might say he had a soft job. I was glad he did and that he didn't have to watch me suffer so much. He would sometimes earn some small pieces of food for doing something extra for people. When he had a little extra, he'd save some for me to have at the end of the day when I returned from work.

The food was in desperately short supply. We had no more weight left on our bodies to lose. Even our skin became thinner from lack of nutrition. The rationed pieces of bread (an eighth of a loaf) were mostly moldy, unfit for consumption. I felt the hunger pains more than ever before. There was a little white dog that belonged to one of the German guards, that used to run around the camp barking. Suddenly it vanished. Later I learned that some of the prisoners killed it for food. Unknowingly, I partook of the dog soup. It might have saved my life.

I mentioned earlier that at the gate entrance, outside the camp, was an SS guard house and a kitchen which was used to prepare meals for the guards. Right next to the kitchen was a garbage pit adjacent to the road, about one hundred feet before the gate entrance. One night as I lay awake thinking, I came up with an idea. This was my idea: After work when the time came for us to fall into ranks for our daily eight mile march back to camp, if I could fall into the beginning ranks, at the extreme right of the column, I would walk right alongside the garbage pit as we passed it. If I could quietly slip into the garbage pit without anyone noticing, I could stuff my pockets with garbage and climb out of the pit before the end of the marching work column reached the gate. Timing was critical. If I did not climb out of the pit in time and was discovered outside the gate after the gates closed, I would have been shot!

I was the smallest and youngest. I thought I had the best chance to succeed. The next evening when we returned from work, I did just that. When the whistle blew at the end of a long hard day to fall in formation, I ran as fast as I could and was one of the first in line. As we neared the camp, I became very nervous. I was risking my life for garbage. A voice inside me said, "You must do it; without this garbage you will certainly starve." As I approached the garbage pit near the gate, most of the German guards turned right to enter the mess hall and get relief from the cold. For all practical purposes, their job was over, we were in camp.

The gates of the camp opened for the work party to enter and I was in the fifth row. I did not want to be in the first row—the SS at the gates would have spotted me immediately. As I neared the open and smelly pit, I quietly slid into the mushy and uninviting hole. I quickly stuffed my pockets with potato peelings and other scraps of food. I hurriedly pulled myself out of the pit in time to join my column at the rear and marched into our camp.

That evening I emptied my pockets to see and

enjoy what delicacies I had acquired, and of course to share them with the others in my barracks. The older prisoners liked me and protected me the best they could. There were some potato peelings, one rotten tomato, frozen pieces of potato, and some scraps of fat. The scraps of fat were the most valuable of all. We could cook it and get a lot of nourishment from it. I grabbed a tin can, went outside and filled it with snow, put the can on the stove until the snow melted, and then delicately introduced the ingredients I procured into the bowl while everyone admiringly and excitedly watched. I spent all evening watching it cook while others kept the fire going. It was a beautiful sight to behold. After it was cooked, I shared it and went to sleep satisfied with my success. I was able to do this several times a week. In recent years, I have reflected on several occasions that it was this extra little bit of food in addition to our daily rations, that saved me, my dad and others from starvation.

I especially recall one evening when I was returning from my cement—carrying job. As I entered the main gate, there was a man looking for me. He watched for me as the column was entering the gate. When he spotted me he yelled out my name and motioned for me to leave the column quickly. I knew this man so I obeyed. He directed me to follow him behind one of the barracks. He told me my dad sent him to inform me that all young people were to be selected and deported. My dad obtained this advanced information from a friendly Capo. He continued by telling me that when the work detail arrived at the main parade ground, that process was to take place. "Your dad wants you to hide for a few hours until the selection process is over." He took me to a distant barracks and hid me under some old blankets. He said "I'll return for you later in the evening." And so it was. Several hours later he returned and took me to my father. It was a happy reunion, to say the least.

All the young people selected at that time were never seen or heard from again. Once again I became the youngest person in the camp!

My dad saw me being pushed beyond my endurance on this strenuous construction job. He looked for a way to get me off this killing work party. The time came when more barbers were needed to cut the hair of the prisoners. In my absence, my dad volunteered me for the job. Dad was a good barber, so he knew how to use a hand operated clipper efficiently. I was assigned to eight barracks of prisoners, to cut hair and also to clean all eight barracks during the day while everyone was working at their cement construction job. Some of the major benefits of my new assignment were not having to march 16 miles to and from work everyday and spending most of the time in a sheltered area. Dad was also previously assigned eight barracks of his own to attend to. In the evenings after all the barracks were attended to, we had to cut hair. We worked until nine or ten at night in order to keep up with the workload. I just couldn't keep up with all the work demanded of me. When my right hand gave out and I could no longer compress the spring of the manually operated clippers, I used both hands together as long as my strength permitted. Everyone's body was lice infested.

The removal of the hair exposed the large nests of lice. It was sickening to watch the lice being squashed between the blades of the clippers. The underarm and pubic areas were the most infested. When Dad was done with his barracks, he'd come over to where I was working and give me a hand. Without Dad's help I surely would have lost my job and would have had to return to carrying sacks of cement.

As a method to reduce the lice epidemic, many people took off their clothes at night and put them on the straw roofs of our barracks. By morning the clothes would be frozen stiff and the lice dead.

The winter was much colder and harsher then usual and the death toll was rising sharply. Many of our fellow prisoners were dying of hunger, frostbite and exhaustion. The remaining prisoners, like myself, were barely able to get about. By now, after almost four years in concentration camps with the most inhumane treatment the Nazis could inflict, we were reduced to skin and bones, like walking skeletons. I saw people walking slowly and suddenly dropping dead. Others died at night. When one awoke next to a dead person it was no shock anymore. It happened so often that we became accustomed to it. I even felt relieved knowing that this person would suffer no more and that where he was going had to be a much better place then what he had here.

My father and I were still two of the somewhat able-bodied prisoners in our camp, perhaps because of the extra nourishment we were able to procure. We were assigned a new job. It was called "the burying detail." The Nazis needed strong people to handle the frozen bodies. Our job was to gather the dead as one would gather litter, with a pushcart. We hauled as many bodies as we could on these two wheeled pushcarts and we pushed and steered the wagon to an open field, where the guards told us to dig a mass grave. Handling and piling the bodies was very difficult. They were frozen stiff and it was impossible to bend the arms and legs to make handling more natural. For tools, we had picks and shovels, but the ground was frozen hard and deep. Every time I'd strike the ground with the heavy pick (which was bigger then I was), I could only break loose the smallest amount of dirt, an ounce or two at the most. Progress was slow. At the end of a ten-hour day of digging, we only got down about eighteen inches. The grave was a six foot cube, 6 x 6 x 6 feet deep. It took us many days to dig one mass grave. At the end of the day's work, we picked up our tools and returned back to camp in the twilight of the last rays of sunlight.

Our cart crew consisted of nine prisoners, three on each side of the cart, two pushing from behind, and one in the front, steering, which was usually me.

We returned to this site for several days, bringing more bodies with us each subsequent day until the grave site was completed. Each day digging became more difficult. The deeper we dug, the harder it was to shovel the dirt. When it was two feet deep, we had to stand on top of one another to exit. We'd back up the pushcart to the open pit and dump as many bodies as possible into it. Some of us were ordered to go down in the grave and do some rearranging to make room for more. That was the time that we feared most. There was always the chance that we'd be shot and left in the pit. We'd pile as many bodies as we could to within twelve inches or so off the ground level, and then shovel a heaping pile of dirt over it. After our job was completed, we'd push our cart to the next camp and start this process all over again. There were many such camps. The camps were scattered several Miles apart. Of course, all the distances were covered on foot, pushing the two—wheeler.

I remember one cold winter morning we went through a small Bavarian town called "Landsberg" with our pushcart. It was a very beautiful small town with curved cobblestone streets and quaint—looking houses and shops lining both sides of the main street. The architecture looked Swiss to me with lots of red tiled roofs. It was the first time in my life that I had seen such architecture. It was so unlike Poland, particularly Grodno.

I wanted to see more of the town and country-side. It seemed so beautiful and peaceful. One would never know that there was a war going on, or that people like us were being enslaved. Some German people opened the windows in their second—story dwellings to look at us as if we were a novelty. We stared at them also. We wanted to get a better look at the people who were doing this to us. The guards pushed us along, preventing us from taking a better look. A German lady threw an apple from her second-story window. One of us caught it. An SS guard saw this and came over and took the apple away from the person who was fortunate enough to catch it.

This was the first time in almost four years,

since the ghetto in Grodno, that we were walking the same streets with civilians in a village or small town atmosphere. The German village people were walking on the sidewalks looking at us, all skin and bones, with our unique blue and white striped prison uniforms, striped cap, and yellow Star of David sewn on the left side of our jackets. They didn't want to get too close to us for fear of contamination or worse. They looked at us as one would at a column of chained prisoners from another country being marched down their main street. The vibrations that reached me were, "I am glad I am not one of them, what kind of strange people are they? I better not get too close, the Nazi guards may cause trouble for me." I felt other messages coming through to me as I made eye contact with these people. "Why is such a small boy wearing a prison uniform? What did he do to get arrested? How could they be walking, they look like corpses? What if they escape—can they hurt us?" My eyes dropped low to the ground. I could not bear the contrast in lifestyles.

A while later as we continued up the hilly street, I managed to lift my eyes again. I saw children playing in the snow and asked myself why they were allowed to play in the snow and have fun, while I was not allowed to even live. It reminded me of how nice it was for people to walk the streets without armed guards on either side of them. I wished that I could go anywhere I wanted to, go straight, turn right or left at my own choosing. The freedom of simple choices, such as when to get up, when to sit, when to walk, where to walk, what kind of work to do, is seldom appreciated. I had forgotten during the past years of being enslaved, how people were supposed to live. All that I had been thinking of during the past years was how to stay alive, where to find food, and how to keep from freezing. I had forgotten that there is more to life than that. We made a right turn onto a new street and saw a large concrete wall that spanned a long distance. We passed a very large, closed gate with Germans standing guard on each side. A man behind me whispered to another, "This is the prison where Hitler was confined and wrote his book *Mein Kampf*. In English it translates as "*My Fight*.." We returned to camp.

It was December 1944, I was almost fourteen years old. The temperature kept dropping fast. The extremities of our bodies were turning white, an indication of frostbite. I kept myself wrapped in as many rags as I could find. Luckily, my feet were small and my shoes were many sizes too large. I had room inside my shoes for much wrapping. I even had room to insert a piece of cardboard in the bottom of my shoes to cover the holes in the soles. I had sufficient rags saved up to cover my ears, nose, and mouth; so did my father. Others were less fortunate. People in our work party walked around with frozen ears, fingers, and toes, and didn't even know it. After the nerve endings die, there is no feeling. We had no choice but to begin breaking apart the wooden bleachers (our beds) in our barracks for burning in that little wood—burning stove located in the center aisle.

I recall one night my father became violently ill with severe stomach pain. His pain was so bad that I felt he could not last the night. He curled up and cried out loud. I became frightened. I had never seen my dad cry like that before, and did not know what I could do to help. I was frightened for him and also for myself. I knew that without him I'd be like a newborn baby left alone in the cold forests of Siberia. The drive for survival prompted me to go into action. I chopped some more wood to make the fire in the stove hotter. I took the burning hot cast—iron lid from the top of the stove and wrapped it in some rags, and held it against my dad's right side, where it hurt. The warmth of the hot lid caused the pain to ease. When I saw it was helping, I went to look for another item that I could be heating on the stove while the stove lid was against dad's stomach. I found a brick and put it on the top of the hot stove. I wanted to have an alternative warm object for when the stove lid cooled. I repeated that process all night and kept the fire going. Dad was not without heat at any time during the night. By morning he felt better and was able to go to work. He had suffered a gallbladder attack. By helping him, I saved his life and possibly mine as well.

Time had been passing slowly and now, several weeks later, the harsh winter was ending and the snow was beginning to melt, causing matters to get worse. The water from the melting snow leaked into our underground barracks and was mixing with the dirt and straw. This caused mud to form all over the floor. From this time on, our feet were always wet and cold. During the evening, we hung the wet rags from our feet, which were used as socks, to dry. Mud was everywhere, including on the bleachers which we slept.

Many more in our ranks were suffering from pneumonia and tuberculosis during this wet spring and many died from these diseases. Our numbers were again dwindling. There were now fewer than one—third the people in Lager #11 than had arrived there almost a year before.

One prisoner pointed toward the mountains and whispered to me in a weak voice, "You see these mountains in the distance. On the other side, just below, is Switzerland and freedom. Just over the hill." I was very interested and understood the geography. I replied to him enthusiastically, "But how do we get there?"

It was now the spring of 1945 and Germany was being crushed by the Allies from all sides. The Nazis tried to destroy the crematorium and gas chambers as they retreated on the Eastern front. Places like **Treblinka, Maidanek**, and **Auschwitz** were already dismantled. The **Dachau** extermination camp was also being deactivated. One of the problems the Nazis now faced was what to do with the remaining prisoners. We found out later that orders came down from Nazi headquarters to destroy the remaining prisoners by any means available and to hide the evidence. What remained of our transport was to be led on a sixty—mile march to the mountainous region of Tyrol and eventually be shot there.

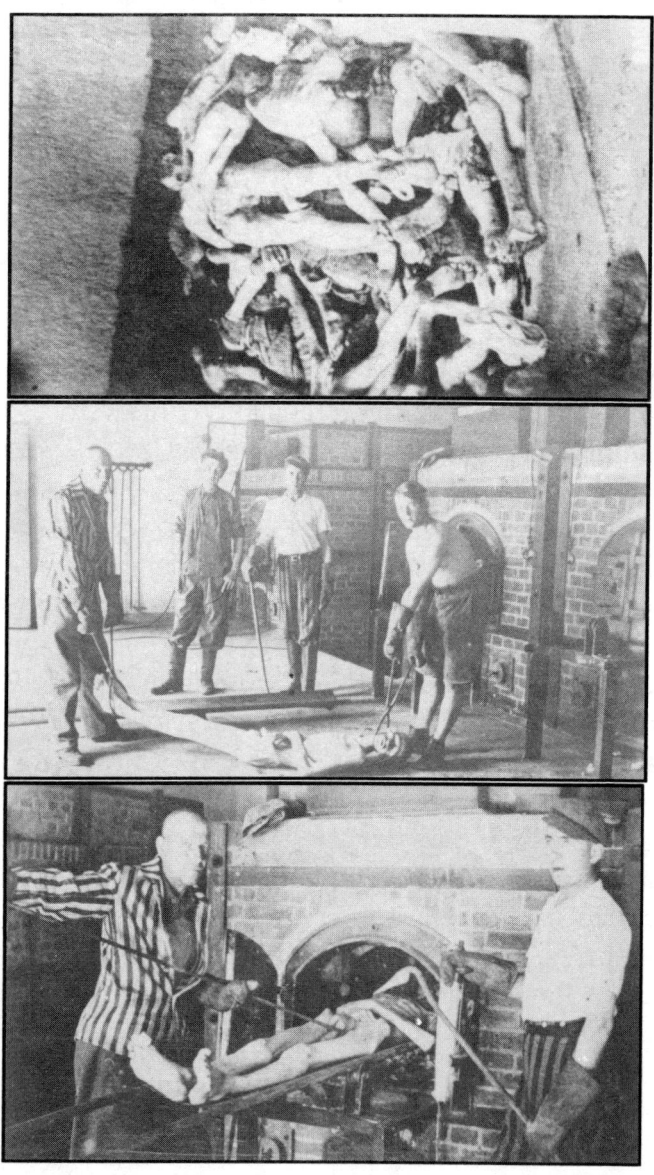

*These photos of 'DACHAU" were given to me by American Soldier who was one of our **Liberating Angels**.*

Chapter 13

Death March, Dachau to Tyrol

We were awakened early one morning at 4:30 a.m. Instead of shouting, "Get up, hurry to work," the Lager Commander requested that everyone take with them all their belongings, that this camp was being closed. We were told that we would move to a new location. Since there were no railroad trains available for us, we had to march on foot to our new destination, which was not very far off.

We quickly complied and wrapped our feet with many rags to hide the holes in our shoes and to protect our feet from the pounding of the road. We were ordered outside for head count. Many SS troops joined us as we turned left and marched toward the main gate. This was *definitely* going to be our last journey. There was no question in our mind of what was going to happen to us on this trip. We began preparing for it mentally the best way we could. Praying was one way. Making wishes was another, such as hoping to join our family in Heaven.

Our column extended for almost a mile. We started out walking rather slowly at first, dragging along what few belongings we possessed, valuables such as a tin plate, tin cup, a few extra rags, and maybe even a blanket. The Nazi guards walked on both sides of the road. There were some Nazi guards on motorbikes, and personnel carriers filled with more SS guards followed behind. As soon as we were out of sight of the camp, a few miles out, the guards began to whip us, shouting "Schnell" (which means fast) in German, causing us to run. While running, we would inadvertently run into each other. The ones who fell were severely beaten. The ones who could get up again and keep up with the column were allowed to do so. The ones who couldn't were later shot by the SS guards who followed. Their bodies were thrown into the ditches along the road. We didn't keep up a steady run. It was run and then walk again. After walking for a few minutes, the shouted command "Run!" was given. It was obvious to all of us that the Nazis did not intend this column to ever reach Tyrol, or at least that they meant to thin it out to a more manageable number. We marched until dusk. At nightfall, our column was marched off the road a few hundred feet and we camped for the night, constantly surrounded by armed guards. At dawn we were awakened and set out to march again. I do not recall any food rations or water being offered to us. We were losing many of our comrades in a day's march. In the evening we'd look around to see who of our friends were missing.

On the third day, we were marching on a narrow road not far from Dachau when suddenly I heard a faint noise in the sky, like an airplane engine. I was the first to hear its sound. I was the youngest and must have had good ears, better than most in our column. I looked up and there, high in the sky, I saw two small, single—engine airplanes. I could barely see them. Some of the guards saw me looking at the sky and also looked up. At the time, our column was passing through a dense forest on both sides of the road. As I was marching, I saw the planes heading

186

straight for us. The SS guards shouted "Hit the ground." In seconds, the two planes buzzed over our column. Almost everyone hit the ground hard and covered their heads. I turned my head and watched. My curiosity took precedence over my safety. I could see the pilots in their cockpits as they zoomed only a few feet over our heads. The plane numbers and U.S. white star insignia were also plainly visible. A great aura of joy surrounded my entire body as the planes vanished high into the sky with incredible speed.

The Germans shouted "Get up!" and made us advance further up the road, where the forest was somewhat more dense. They were hoping that the pilots would not see the column if we were on the road nearer to the pine trees. This turned out to be a big mistake for the SS and eventual freedom for my dad and me. Here is what happened. The Allied pilots easily recognized us as being prisoners by our striped blue and white uniforms and had decided to make a second pass at the column to disrupt the Nazi control over us. Within minutes, out of nowhere, the two airplanes appeared again from behind with screaming engines and the sun behind them, roaring right over our heads. This time they dropped two bombs on the road, one in front of the column and the second at the rear. The planes strafed the Nazi guards on both sides of the road as the guards shouted to us, "Hit the ground." They themselves hid at the lowest part of the ditches along both sides of the road. I was still standing there in amazement. Some of the prisoners, including my dad and me, saw all the Nazi guards lying in the ditches below ground level with their heads covered. We utilized this once—in—a—lifetime momentous opportunity and started running toward the safety of the trees, in the nearby forest. The guards were still lying in the ditches, seeking safety from the planes' noisy machine—gun bullets. The forest was located about three hundred feet off the road. I was moving as fast as my legs could carry me, looking at my dad, making sure he was still with me. By the time the guards got up, my dad and I were halfway there. The guards shouted "Zurick!" meaning "Return or we'll shoot," and they began firing at us. Most of the escapees stopped and returned to the column as the guards ordered, but my dad and I, and a handful of others, continued running toward the safety of the trees. We expected to be hit by bullets at any moment. The two American planes made one more pass strafing the guards and disappeared high in the sky. That extra pass gave us the additional moments necessary to reach the forest edge and apparent safety.

The guards could not take time to go look for us in the dense forest. They had to advance the rest of the column to its destination in Tyrol and the eventual end. Besides, they felt that we would be caught soon enough. There was nowhere for us to go in our striped prison uniforms, in the middle of Germany. Once I reached the forest I felt somewhat safer, but I still kept running deeper and deeper as far as my legs would carry me. I did not know whether the guards would return to look for us. When I could run no more, I fell to the ground and rested alongside a pine tree. My dad was within my sight, a little behind. We spent that night in the forest. It was a cold night, even though it was already the second day of

May, 1945. I kept thinking, *"If I survive the war, will I ever have the opportunity to thank those pilots for saving my life? If I can't find them, how will they ever know?"*

We spent the rest of the late afternoon and evening resting and getting a little sleep among the trees. It was a very cold and scary night. We were without guards, but also without freedom. It was the first time in many years that we were not accounted for. Up until yesterday, the authorities knew at all times where we were. All of our decisions were made for us. All we had to do was obey orders. Suddenly we had to begin making decisions ourselves.

The next day was May 3, 1945. We spent most of the day familiarizing ourselves with the handful of prisoners that were among us, observing the road for troop movements, and picking berries and mush-rooms to fill our empty stomachs. We still didn't know exactly where we were geographically or whether the war was still continuing. Each one of us had a different idea of our location and what our next course of action ought to be. Some felt that we ought to leave the forest and find a farm where we might get something to eat. Others felt that we ought to watch for Germans on the road, kill them, and take their clothes for our own use so that we might cover great distances on foot without being detected, while some felt that we should remain here until we could agree on a firm plan.

We spent two more days and two more nights in this forest and no one had yet come looking for us. We drank the water from shaded puddles that remained from previous rains and melting snow.

Along the road there was no movement of people or vehicles. It seemed strange. I felt that something was happening. In the past there was always at least troop movement on the road, with soldiers coming and going in all directions. At nightfall, we picked a soft spot of ground alongside a large pine tree, gathered some long pine needles for extra comfort, and tried to get another night's sleep. We hadn't removed our clothes since we left Lager #11 several days before, but that was the least of our worries.

Early, on the next morning of May 5, 1945, I heard some faint engine noises in the distance. At this time, I was the only one who heard the sounds. I said to my dad, "What is this noise that we hear?" He replied, "I can't hear anything." I said to him, "Please be very quiet and put your ear to the ground." He did, and a few minutes later others had awakened and were also hearing a rumbling. We cautiously advanced to near the edge of the forest, where we could look out to the road but could not be seen, and we watched and listened. With each passing minute, the sound became louder and closer. I could now hear the chains clatter on the spokes of the wheels, as on a tank or self—propelled artillery. Everyone was scared and tense. We thought that the SS finally were returning to look for us in the forest. As we looked far to the left of the road, from the direction we had come, we noticed a column of tanks advancing slowly toward us on the same road that we were marching on just a few days before. The tanks were evenly spaced, and on some of the turrets I could see that the hatch covers were open and some heads were visible to me. As the tank column reached the vicinity of the forest, the hatch covers closed and the heads of the gunners were no longer visible to me. The tanks looked strange. The German cross was missing and in its place was a large white star painted on the tank. *We suddenly realized that these were not German tanks.* Uncontrollably, we left the safety of the forest and began eagerly running toward the tanks. We were dressed in our blue and white striped prison uniforms and prison caps. It didn't take the Americans long to discover that we were prisoners and were seeking their help.

When we finally approached the tanks they stopped the column for us. They saw how starved we were and immediately shared their rations with us, giving us such goodies as canned cheese and crackers, chocolate bars, and oranges. We could not communicate with the Americans and they could not communicate with us, but you have never seen a happier reunion. With their help we jumped on the tanks and began hugging and hand shaking. I pointed to my mouth as one American soldier looked at me. He gave me some rations and also a chocolate bar. That was the first chocolate that I had seen in more than four years. Our stomachs were not used to this rich food, so as a result many of us got sick and some even died. It was especially sad to see some of our friends make it to the end and then die from eating. The only comfort we derived was that at least they died in freedom.

It was General Patton's armored division that liberated us. Luckily for me, one of the American soldiers spoke Polish. He was from Chicago. I was able to communicate with him and he acted as translator to all of us. I could not believe that we were no longer surrounded by hostile Nazi guards, and instead befriended by a battalion of friendly American soldiers. My father and I began to weep tears of joy. We cried for a long time; we couldn't stop. It was a release from tensions that had been building in us all these years. I felt so good. It felt as if the weight of a tank was lifted from my chest and I could breathe again. At last the long nightmare was over. We couldn't believe that we had made it. The feeling of happiness that fell upon me was one that can not ever be described or compared. It was like being born at age 15. The only way I can best describe it is by mentioning what it was *not* like: It wasn't like getting a new car, or winning a big jackpot. Not like graduating from college, or getting a big job. The joys that I have just described happen to many people, and if missed once they can happen again. The feeling of sudden freedom as compared to certain death is truly indescribable. Prior to the union with the American troops, I accepted the fact that I would die before my sixteenth birthday and thanked God for the years He had given me with my family and friends. When in Auschwitz, I considered myself dead, watching the last sunrise every day. On this day of liberation, I looked up at the sky from the top of an American tank and said, "Thank you, God, for giving me extra time. I will be grateful for each additional day that You will let me live and I will consider it a *bonus*, a special *gift* from **You**."

Chapter 14

Germany After The War

"Come with us," said the Polish—speaking American soldier. "We will take you to a camp where other prisoners were liberated and you can stay there." (It was called a "DP" camp, or "Displaced Persons" camp). "We will give you clothing and food until you decide what to do and where to go." We agreed and we went with them, riding on top of the tank for the short journey to a former concentration camp, which was now a camp for displaced prisoners. The ride on top of an American tank moments after liberation had to be the *greatest ride of a lifetime.* Nothing could have thrilled me more at that moment. No plane, speedboat, or sports car could equal the exuberance of that moment. This time, the *gates were open* and there were no Nazi guards around us. We could come and go at will. In this camp, we met other prisoners who were also liberated, and it was interesting to talk to them about their native countries and how they, too, managed to survive. It was on the third day of our freedom, May 8, 1945, that we learned from our new American friends that the war had finally ended. There was great celebration and much jubilation. *We laughed and cried simultaneously with disbelief!*

Dad and I tried to find out if anyone had seen my mother and brother; no success. We met Jewish people from all over Europe and even a few from our town of Grodno.

This DP camp was operated by the "ORT" organization, a volunteer charitable society which helped locate missing family and provide temporary life necessities. Vocational classes were organized and I enrolled to take mechanic and machinist courses which I successfully completed several months later.

The sudden availability of better food agreed with me and I grew stronger each day. I felt the urge to learn anything and everything, to make up for five years of deprived education which had just ended. I began learning German and read everything that I could focus my mind on. A surge of energy entered my body the day I was freed and I began soaking up information like a sponge. There was so much that I had missed and needed to catch up on.

During these months, we began writing letters to my uncles on my mother's side in Israel and to uncles on my father's side in America. We assumed that if any of our relatives in Europe survived, they would be contacting these relatives in foreign countries. After months of corresponding, the results were negative. We still did not give up hope, even though it appeared hopeless.

To our amazement we did receive a letter from my dad's oldest brother that he and his two sons (my cousins) managed to survive the war by escaping to Russia with the Russian army as they retreated in 1941. They miraculously made it to Israel, but only after spending some time in Siberia, because they were accused of being spies. While in Siberian camps, they met my uncle, David Burder, who was married to my mother's younger sister. He was the one who was always ill with an ulcer. While briefly serving in the Polish Army, he was taken prisoner by the Russians and sent to Siberia also. How a sick man like him survived the cold and hardship in Siberia and made it mostly on foot to Israel is more remarkable than I can imagine.

Two months had passed and the time had come for us to move on. Dad and I were no longer comfortable being fed and clothed. We needed to go out and make our own way in this new world. The urge to leave the barracks and the familiar barbed wire fences became overwhelming.

We took our belongings and walked through the open gates of the DP camp in our newly acquired civilian clothes. We set out on foot in search of a new land and new life. There was no future for us here and none awaited us in Poland either. To the best of our knowledge, none of our friends and relatives had survived. We took the gravel road from camp for a couple of miles to the main paved road. When we got there, we couldn't even decide whether to go to the left or to the right. We saw American transports going to the right, so we based our decision on the truck movements. It felt wonderful seeing friendly troops all around, knowing that no one would harm us. We had walked for several hours and our feet were getting tired. We were making good time and were hoping that we would reach a city or a town by nightfall and find a place to sleep. Fear once again fell upon us as we walked. We began to have second thoughts about leaving our DP camp. We had no idea where we were going or what we would find there. We had no money—it was worthless anyway.

We had nothing of value to pay for food or shelter. We couldn't even speak German well enough to communicate with the civilian population.

During late afternoon as we were beginning to panic, we noticed a community far off in the distance. We picked up our pace and began walking much faster in that direction. The road became wider and we could read the name of the street, "Dachauer Strasse." That name was very familiar to us. It brought back painful memories, but we couldn't let it interfere with our most recent joy of liberation and so quickly removed them from our thoughts. An hour later we were at Mosach, a suburb on the outskirts of Munich.

I had already added almost twenty miles to the soles of my oversized shoes since we left the security of the DP camp. My legs were tired and weak, and I could hardly go on any further. The need for rest and sleep were equally urgent. As we walked through the city, all we saw was rubble and devastation. The city of Munich along Dachauer Strasse was completely leveled. All the brick buildings in sight were leveled. We saw an occasional brick chimney still standing. We walked for many blocks and every building, without exception, was bombed or burned. It appeared that there were no German survivors in the city. We wondered what happened to all the German people. We continued walking through the rubble—filled streets. On our way, we passed a tall, bombed building where all the windows were broken. Some windows were at street level. I bent down to see what was in the cellar and saw thousands of wine bottles. Most were empty and some were filled with wine. My dad lowered me through the small window into the cellar to scout around, hoping that I would find some food. To our disappointment, there was none to be found. We realized that the building we were in was a winery. I shouted to my dad that this might be a good place to spend the night and he joined me inside.

We made ourselves comfortable on the concrete floor. We selected and opened a bottle of wine, shared it, and fell asleep quickly, due to fatigue, exhaustion, and the effect of our liquid meal.

We awoke early the next morning at daybreak and had another bottle of wine for breakfast, not because we liked wine but because there was nothing else for us to eat or drink, not even water. The water system was damaged in the bombings.

I was over fifteen years old and not yet very tall. I wore adult pants, size 38 x 33, that were bunched up in the back to take up the slack and held up by a rope that I used for a belt. The cuffs of my pants were rolled up several times to prevent them from dragging on the ground. I wore a man size dress shirt tucked into my baggy pants and a large long overcoat with many pockets. Those were the only civilian clothes I could find. I had no jacket. Wearing something with many pockets was very useful—I had found this out before in the KZs. I dressed that way not to look ridiculous but because no other option was available to me. I wore all the personal belongings I possessed.

It was time to face the uncertainty of a new day. I stuffed several wine bottles into the pockets of my overcoat; Dad did the same. We crawled out through the same window through which we had entered. We began walking toward the center of the city, hoping to find someone with food who would be willing to trade for wine. I must have looked ridiculous with all of the wine bottles sticking out of my pockets.

Soon we came upon a site where an American battalion had set up camp. We stopped and wanted to trade with the soldiers, but we could not speak English and the soldiers could not speak Polish. It was just impossible to communicate. My dad gave a bottle of wine to the soldier and pointed to his mouth, meaning food, hunger. Finally he got the message and gave us bread and cheese. This was the first time I saw fresh white bread in many years and what a beautiful sight it was! We began eating very rapidly and the American soldier couldn't get over the extent of our hunger. When we were done eating the food he gave us, he offered us more. We eagerly accepted more, not knowing when and where we would get our next meal. As we left, I noticed a crate of oranges near the door. I squatted quickly and put an orange into one of my empty pockets, unobserved. It was impossible for me to resist such an abundance of oranges, having not even seen the color orange for so many years. Later I asked myself why I stole that orange from the American who fed me just minutes before. I was very upset with myself for doing such a thing. I realized that my action was wrong and vowed I would never do this again.

We left the American battalion and spent many more hours walking through the ghost city of Munich, finding nothing and seeing no one. What was left of the German population must have been in hiding. Having nowhere else to go, we returned to the wine cellar where we stayed the night before. We browsed through the winery and discovered an abandoned bunkhouse, and there we made our new home.

The following day, we returned to the site of the American battalion where we had eaten the day before. Luckily for us, Dad found an American soldier who could speak Polish. That opened up a whole new world for us. Many soldiers had questions for us. The Polish—speaking soldier was able to translate and other soldiers were beginning to communicate with us also. Of course they gave us more food and we gave them Mösel wine. Dad informed them that he was a barber by trade and could cut their hair and give them shaves. They accepted my offer to do KP duty for them. I was happy to do it just to be around the food.

One day as I was walking along the deserted streets of München, I came across a building that resembled a fire station. I went over and tried the gate. It was open. I looked inside, and there I saw two of the most beautiful red fire engines. The building was unguarded and there was no one inside. I climbed on the engine and studied all the instruments. It was exciting. When I was done, I saw a shiny Moped also parked inside. I raised the rear wheel up on the stand and began to pedal. I released the clutch and the engine started. I opened the door and drove it outside. There was gas in it. I drove it all over town and it was great having all that power (50 horsepower) at my command. The next day I drove it past an MP directing traffic. He called me over and took it away. I reverted to exploring on foot.

A new and wonderful world began to unfold before us. Dad and I were enthusiastic workers and the soldiers liked our very willing attitude to please. We had a steady job, so to speak. Dad became the battalion barber and I helped mostly in the kitchen. For the first time in years we had all the food we could eat. We didn't know when to stop eating. I couldn't bear to see so much good food being wasted. Dad received tips and I shined boots in my spare time to earn money. I usually had a few spare hours between meals when I would set out on my own, exploring the city. After a few weeks, German civilians began walking the streets and the newly—repaired streetcars began traveling the city. All the building sites were still rubble, but the streets were cleared and navigable.

I used to rush to finish the pots and pans after each meal so that I could ride the streetcars. I really enjoyed riding them. I was able to see so much of the city in a short time. I had American occupation money and could buy things available in the few shopping areas not completely destroyed by the bombing. The first thing I bought myself was a pair of pants and a shirt that fit me. It was such a great feeling to wear something that fit well. I ate as well as the American soldiers. I became strong and began to grow taller. Everyone told me how well I looked, and that boosted my morale.

Most of the German civilian population were still starving. Food supplies were in great demand. At our battalion kitchen, much of the excess food was discarded after each meal. I asked the head cook if I could have the leftovers that were destined for the garbage cans. He said "sure." I began saving the excess food and stored it in empty one gallon ration cans. I was able to accumulate several cans full of food after each meal. When my KP duty was finished, I would take two of these cans at a time, puncture a small hole at the top of each side of the can and thread a string through if for a handle. I would take two cans on the streetcar with me and soon I would trade it to the Germans for some valuable article or cash. After both cans were sold, I'd return to base, pick up two more cans of leftover food, and do it again. The American soldiers eagerly bought whatever articles I had acquired that day. They had money and nothing to spend it on. It worked out well for all of us.

One day, while out selling leftover food on the street, I met a German lady who bought some of my food. She questioned me about where I was getting the food, and also about where I lived. I told her that my father and I lived in a bombed out winery on Dachauer Strasse. She informed me that she had an extra bedroom in her house that she'd be willing to rent to my dad and me just for food. Her husband died on the Russian front and she lived in Mosach with her mother and two small children. It was very close, walking distance to where Dad and I worked. I told her that I'd discuss it with my father and took her address. We moved in there a few days later.

She lived in a very small but clean house and we had a very small bedroom with one bed and barely enough room for a chair and small dresser. Dad and I slept together in the clean, soft bed with nice white linen. It was the best bed that we ever slept in. Although the comforts that were available to us were greater than those we ever had before, we could not justify living in a German home after what we had been through. We soon found a vacant apartment in a large apartment building a block away and moved there. Many of the units were bombed out. Ours was intact and on the second floor.

Dad and I made arrangements with the Polish-speaking American soldier to send our money to my uncle in Los Angeles. This is how it was done: When Dad and I got a few occupation dollars and coins together, we'd give it to our soldier friend, who would send it to his father in Chicago. His father would write a check and send it to my uncle in Los Angeles. After one year's time, we had accumulated $1,200.00 U.S. dollars in America. In 1945, it represented a nice sum of cash. We corresponded frequently with Uncle Julius in Los Angeles and we knew that all the deposits were forwarded.

We continued to correspond with my uncles Joshua and Label in Palestine and also with Uncle Julius in Los Angeles. We still had hopes that my mother and brother were alive somewhere and didn't know how to find us. This thought never left our minds. We saw other people being reunited with their loved ones. It was a matter of more time until I would find my mother and brother, as some others had, I thought.

We needed a permanent home to continue with our new lives. We couldn't stay in Germany. This land was soaked with the blood of millions of our people. We didn't want to return to Poland either—that was under Russian rule. There was nothing for us in Poland. All of our people were deported. The thought of being the only Jews in Grodno was unacceptable to us. There were only two places for us to consider: America or Palestine.

We vigorously proceeded to make plans to leave this war—torn land. Through Jewish organizations, we applied to emigrate to Palestine, even though the British did not allow survivors into Palestine. Many of our people, having no other choice, risked their lives to emigrate to Palestine illegally. Uncle Julius was sponsoring us for emigration to America. He had to guarantee that he would be responsible for our welfare and that we would not become a burden to the U.S. Government. The immigration quota was still very small and it was difficult to get a visa.

I can't recall exactly why, but we had to move from our apartment. I think it was condemned for being unsafe, weakened by bomb damage.

Berl Lom, my dad's friend who once accused me of cutting off his pocket and stealing his bread ration, survived and found us in München. I wasn't particularly fond of him since he falsely accused me and never accepted my true statement. He had completely forgotten that incident, but it still bothered me. Berl began dealing in the black market and somehow managed to get us some needed commodities. Little by little, more survivors showed up and we began living and socializing together in the evenings and on weekends.

I was approaching my sixteenth birthday and my dad and others decided to make me a party. They invited many of their friends and threw a beautiful party with plenty of food and liquor. I was still the youngest, and there wasn't anyone my age to have fun with. All the adults had a good time eating and drinking. No one paid any attention to me even though the party was supposed to be in my honor. They offered me liquor and said to me, "Come, Hirshel, drink and have a good time." I sat there by the piano alone, crying for my mother and brother, wishing that the party would end.

Almost a whole year had passed and we were still in Germany. None of our immigration documents had come through. We returned to live in the small bunkhouse by the winery. We were joined by two other young men who were survivors from a different city, and a cousin of my dad's from Grodno; her name was Lona. She had lost all her family so she moved in with us. She sort of kept the little house clean and washed our clothes on occasion. She attached herself to us and also applied for visas to go with us wherever we chose to go. It appeared that no western country wanted to let us immigrate. I believe that the United States was one of the few countries that agreed to let us in.

Finally, we opened the mail one day and found a letter from America. It contained the papers we were waiting for, our visa and travel documents. It stated that we should report to Bremerhaven within a few days to sail to America on a transport troopship called "Marine Marlin." We were overjoyed and began hastily packing our belongings. That very same afternoon, a big truck came by our dwelling. There were many people in the back already. The driver shouted to us, "Everyone who wants to go to Palestine, jump on."

What an enormous decision to have to make on a moment's notice. It's true that going to Palestine would be our first choice, but getting to Palestine was extremely difficult. It was under British mandate and no Jewish immigrants were allowed. It meant being smuggled to Cypress and waiting for an illegal ship to make the dangerous crossing. Being caught by the British would mean more imprisonment in barbed wire detention camps. In spite of the dangers, our need for a Jewish homeland was strong. After being rejected by so many nations, Palestine was the only logical place to go. It would be a place where we could have our own identity and be free at last among our own people.

Before us was a direct journey to America. Our documents were in order, with a paid—for steamship ticket in our hands. We could enter the U.S.A. legally and become U.S. citizens in time, with all human rights guaranteed by the constitution. A new land unmarked by the recent war was on our horizon.

The truck engine was still idling and the driver shouted once more, "Anyone wishing to go to Palestine, jump on, we don't have all day." Many threw their belongings onto the back of the truck and jumped on. I said to my dad, "Can we go to America, since we can enter the country easily and legally? If we find that we don't like it there, maybe we can go to Palestine later."

We made our decision to go to America in less than a minute, and watched the truck take off in a cloud of dust.

Eight months before, my father had a suit made for me by a tailor and he bought me a brand new pair of dress shoes for my trip. I was not allowed to wear the suit or the new shoes. When the time came to try them on, they were too small. I had outgrown both the suit and the shoes. What a waste. I felt bad that I had nothing new to wear on my trip. My dad and his cousin Lona had new clothes made and were well dressed and stylish.

I recalled that even in my native town of Grodno, my brother and I used to walk well ahead of my parents because we lacked suitable attire. I was sixteen years old now and appearance became important to me. I was beginning to notice girls and didn't want to dress ridiculously. For the first time in my life, I became conscious of my image and it became a burden to me. My dad wasn't sensitive to my feelings and his cousin Lona couldn't care less.

The happy thought of leaving Germany took precedence in my mind and I began to concentrate more on the preparation of the journey and beyond.

As per explicit instructions, we took the train to Bremerhaven where our ship would be waiting. This was a passenger train with velvet seats on both sides of the aisle and large glass windows all the way to the ceiling. We each had one suitcase. My dad had put leather belts around his and Lona's suitcases to prevent them from popping open. My little suitcase was tied with a thin rope like a ribbon around my birthday present. Dad didn't have any more leather belts and I understood this.

The train ride to Bremerhaven was exciting. The seats were soft and fluffy, with clean towels on the headpiece. The ride was smooth and soft, like floating on a cloud. I had a window seat and looked at everything as the train travelled through the countryside. The train picked up speed as it left the city and the rhythmic clatter calmed my nerves. I began thinking of my previous train rides in box cars to various concentration camps. I didn't want to think about that. I shook my head vigorously and began concentrating on the beautiful countryside passing in front of me like a moving art exhibit.

The train ride from Munich to Bremerhaven was long. Every few hours or so, the train stopped to take on more passengers. Most of the passengers were old women and small children. When the train became crowded and there were no more seats, I felt obligated to give my seat to an older lady, even though I knew she was German. I offered my seat to an elderly lady who was holding the hand of a young granddaughter, about fifteen years old. They both took the seat that I had vacated. I stood in front of them holding on to one of the leather straps hanging from the ceiling. Not a word was spoken. The old lady smiled slightly informing me that she was pleased by my gesture.

It was almost dusk and the sun's rays filtered through the opposite window, illuminating the faces of these two women. I was amazed by the contrast in their facial appearance, comparing the old and the young. I had never been so close to a young girl before and I was beginning to feel uncomfortable. It was also getting very warm in the car and many of the passengers were falling asleep in their seats. Suddenly the train engineer must have applied the brake. The train slowed with a screech from the wheels rubbing against the rails. Most people standing fell in a forward direction. I was standing in front of the young girl and her grandmother. I bent my knee forward to prevent me from falling on the young girl and my thigh became wedged between the girls knees momentarily. When I recovered and she moved her knees together I realized that we had both for the first time became aware of a strange new feeling. Not a word was ever spoken between us. By morning we were entering the railroad station of Bremen and disembarked. The young girl left with her grandmother, and I picked up my little suitcase and followed my dad to the information booth.

Our documents were carefully checked by immigration. I had to remove the rope from my suitcase for inspection. I was embarrassed traveling with such shabby luggage. Inside my luggage they found nothing of value, only some dishes, cooking pots, and old clothes. I think that the customs officer was also embarrassed with my contents and permitted Dad and Lona to pass unchecked.

It was a great feeling going through the customs line and finding myself standing on the other side of the gate. I turned around and took a last look behind me. In my mind I said "Goodbye, Germany, I never want to see you again." We followed the marked path to the exterior of the building and up the ramp to our waiting ship.

Chapter 15

Aboard Ship to the U.S.A.

The three of us—Dad, Lona, and I—walked up to the dock, and there before me was the most beautiful ship in the world. It was painted gray and across its bow, in large white letters, was the name *"MARINE MARLIN."* It was many stories tall and its displacement was 20,000 tons. This was the ship that was to take us to a new continent and hopefully a new life where we could live in freedom.

The ship was well guarded. There was a narrow gangway along the side reaching all the way up to the third deck. Two U.S. Navy personnel stood at the top near a small oval door. At the bottom of the gangway were two more Navy personnel checking for IDs and travel documents. We presented our papers and were quickly instructed to go aboard. What a wonderful feeling it was to come aboard the ship legally. We were ushered to the third or fourth level below. The metal staircase was narrow and steep. It was not a luxury ship. It was a troop transport designed to carry many soldiers. We reached our deck and we were each assigned a bunk.

Our quarters were very crowded. The bunks were stacked five or six high with only about eighteen inches between bunks. The rows of bunks were spaced close together, making the aisles narrow. It felt like being inside a submarine. The temperature below was very warm even though the ventilating fans were operating. The ship was very large. I wanted to go topside but was afraid of getting lost. I tried hard to memorize the passages and stairways that led to our quarters. After settling in our quarters and putting my belongings under my pillow, I got up the confidence to go topside to get some fresh air and watch people boarding.

Just being on board and looking down on the dock felt like being in heaven, severed from this European continent. I couldn't wait for the engines to start and for us to be on our way. We had no idea when this ship would be sailing. Some said this afternoon, while others said not until tomorrow. There was this nagging feeling that we were not yet completely safe until the ship sailed. Something could still go wrong we felt, perhaps too many people on the ship, or papers not in order.

Instructions were given to us over the ship's PA system, such as not to move about too much, and what time meals would be served in the dining room for various quarters. I had to listen very carefully to the instructions. I could understand some English, but not if it was spoken too fast. I translated the English to Yiddish for my father. He was much slower in picking up the language. I heard an announcement that dinner would be served at 6:00 p.m. for our quarters in the starboard dining room on the second level. We arrived at the dining room at 6:00p.m. sharp, ready to partake of our shipboard dinner.

It was a large, open hall. There were many rows of long dining tables close together with benches on both sides. At the center of each table were one—gallon jars of peanut butter, apple butter, orange marmalade, and sugar. Near the entrance was a large stack of GI stainless steel trays and silverware. Right next to the tray stack was a cafeteria—style food line with GI cooks doing the serving. The food looked excellent. I filled my tray and followed my dad to a vacant bench. I recall saying to my dad, "doesn't anybody steal all that marmalade?" It was difficult for me to understand how these items could be left so unattended. We ate a lot and went to bed early. It was a long, tiring, exciting day.

The sleeping quarters were very crowded and the temperature was hot and muggy because so many people were on the ship. The noisy ventilating fans could not provide sufficient cool air for comfort. W e all removed most of our clothing and tried to get a good night's sleep, suspended in our bunks.

Morning came all too soon. We heard the wake—up call for breakfast. We got dressed and went to the large latrine, where many people could be accommodated at once. It was a very large room with many sinks and toilets lined up in rows along the walls. I was amazed the way the waste water was sucked down the sink like a vacuum. First the men went in and then the same latrine was used by the women.

We walked up three decks and were right at the main door of the mess hall. The breakfast was excellent. There were three types of juice, scrambled eggs, pancakes, canned fruit, and dry cereal. That was the first time I was introduced to an instant breakfast. We could take as much as we wanted of anything, and we could even go back for seconds if we wanted to.

We had free movement around the ship except for the engine room, the upper deck, and the bridge. I spent most of the morning exploring the ship. Lunch was served in the same mess hall and the food was superb. We were being fed like the American soldiers and we all knew that the American soldier was the best fed soldier in the world.

In the early afternoon, as I looked over the side of the ship, I noticed a lot of activity. It appeared that we were about to cast off. I went to look for my father to share the excitement of the departure with me. I found him below and pulled him by the hand topside to enjoy the activities with me. Lona also came along. The deck became filled with many people sharing the same idea. I took a space in front at the railing where I could have an unobstructed view of the departure. I learned earlier in the concentration camps the art of selecting a space where you want to be at a given time. This habit has remained with me to this day. When I enter a restaurant or a theater I always select the best location even though others are offered to me. It took two more hours to finish loading the ship with supplies, remove the gangway, and release the ropes. A tugboat arrived on the scene and began pushing the boat away from the dock. Soon another tugboat joined the scene, and it appeared that the pier slowly began to pull away from the ship. The water between the ship and pier was churning vigorously as the people and objects at the pier appeared smaller in the distance.

We heard a loud roar as the ship's main

engines started up and we saw the wake at the bow indicating that we were moving under our own power. Everyone topside was waving goodbye as the European continent was disappearing in the distance. I looked at it for the last time. It felt good leaving this blood—drenched land once and for all, wanting never to return. As the land disappeared from view, I turned my head and my thoughts were directed toward the endless sea horizon. This was the first time in my life that I could see no land over a body of water—the first time I saw a horizon at sea. My future and America were somewhere out there in the distance; there was land that my eyes were longing to see. I wondered what this new land would be like, wondering whether it would have similar landscape, trees, and rivers; whether the people would like us, and most of all, I wondered how we would communicate, not speaking English well. I knew instantly that learning English must become my main priority. I engaged everyone I could in English conversation, particularly the American sailors. I asked them all sorts of questions in my broken English. I deliberately forced them to speak with me.

The sun was setting in the west and was practically touching the water on the horizon when I noticed a large ship about a mile or two in front of us. I looked to the stern and saw another large ship about the same distance behind us. I asked the sailors about the other ships and was informed that we were traveling in a convoy of five ships.

The next morning I got up early and went topside. We were surrounded by a large rough sea, no land anywhere in sight. The swells were about four to eight feet high. I could still see in the distance two other ships from our convoy bobbing in the water. I met a Russian girl standing on deck, leaning against the rail, watching the stern break the waves and churning white water. She was dressed in a large gray overcoat and wore a babushka over her head. She was a couple of years older than me and that made her look like a mature woman. Her face, what you could see of it, was very pretty. A very small nose and rounded face. She had a faraway look in her eyes, probably reflecting on the past and wondering what was awaiting her in America. Our ship was beginning to roll and bob up and down. The wind was cold with a wet mist in the air hitting my face. It was really too cold for anyone to be topside. Except for her, I was the only one out there. I was about twenty feet from her when I began walking in her direction while holding onto the guard rail. She noticed me approaching and looked up smiling. I said to her *"Dobra Dziena"* in Russian, which means (good day). "My name is Gregory, what is yours?" "Sonia," she replied. I knew Russian from going to a Russian school for two years, from 1939 to 1941 while we were under Russian occupation in Poland. Gregory was my Russian name, which is why I used it to introduce myself to her. It would be more familiar to her and less threatening. Sonia was glad that I could speak her language and we conversed for a long time.

Our conversation consisted mostly of family backgrounds. I was too shy to talk about anything else. She was traveling with her mother to America to live with her grandparents who had emigrated

long ago. Her father was killed in the Ukraine by
Nazis during the war. We had something in common. We both hated the Nazis for killing our relatives. We began to run out of things to talk about.

It turned very cold, and it was time for me to
go below and check in with my dad. The sea became
very stormy that night and many people began to get
seasick. The ship began rolling from side to side as
well as bobbing up and down. The swells increased in
size from the day before. We were heading into a
major storm. By morning the sea became even
rougher and everything on the ship that wasn't tied
down was moving. Most people stayed in their
bunks, too sick to get about. I went topside and was
immediately splashed by a big wave. The wind
velocity increased and it was raining. I saw Sonia
standing at the railing in a red waterproof raincoat
and a leather rain hat over her head. I said to her,
"What are you doing here, you'll get blown over-
board." She replied, "I like to feel the wind and
splashing sea on my face. I'll be OK." I said "I'll see
you later." I went below to look in on my dad and the
others who were too sick to get up and about. The
weather continued to worsen and by late afternoon
the entire convoy decided to change course and
turned around 180° in an attempt to avoid the storm.

For two days and two nights we traveled east at
18 knots, losing precious time. Even though it wasn't
true, it felt like a nightmare, returning to Germany.

By the end of the second day traveling in the
wrong direction, the sea was much calmer, the winds
and rain subsided, and the convoy turned around,
heading west toward America once more. The wel-

come news was joyful, and everyone began feeling somewhat better. Very few people showed up in the dining room for meals during the storm. Fortunately, I did not get seasick and enjoyed as much food as I could eat. I had never seen so much food prepared in my life as was available in this mess hall. It was strange for me to remember that only a short time ago thousands of our people died of starvation. I quickly turned my train of thought toward the future and more pleasant opportunities that might be available to me in the new land.

The temperature below was still high. The air conditioning was inadequate for such a large passenger load. Topside was still my favorite place to be. I got up at dawn and went topside. The weather was calm and clear. The ocean was almost smooth with swells only two to four feet. A gentle, cool breeze kept the flag waving. As I looked to the south, I could see a ship passing on the horizon. It was a beautiful sight watching the smoke stacks emitting black smoke, giving evidence that there was life out there. After four days at sea without a passing ship, it was a most welcome sight. I watched until the ship was no longer visible: then I went down to the mess hall for an enormous breakfast: GI—style scrambled eggs, bacon, sausage, French toast, pancakes, orange juice, coffee, milk, biscuits, and of course, the usual one—gallon jars of apple butter, orange marmalade, and peanut butter. We had practically the same breakfast every day with only slight variations. As always, we could go back for seconds.

I had already explored every nook and cranny on the ship that was accessible to passengers and I knew my way around pretty well. One place which I really wanted to see was the engine room. Having completed auto mechanic school and machinist school, it was of special interest to me. That was off limits however, and I had to do without seeing it.

Aside from exploring, I passed the time by participating in fire drills, walking the decks, and learning English, which was soon to be my language.

The sixth day at sea had arrived and we could still see no land. I was beginning to wonder if America really existed, never before realizing that the world was so large. As I walked the deck, I again came upon my friend Sonia, standing against the railing, dressed in a typical Russian peasant outfit. I walked up to her nervously saying, "How are you, it is good to see you again." She replied "Much better now, but I was very sick during the storm." I said, "That's probably why I did not see you the last few days." I moved closer to her, holding on to the railing. I deliberately slid my little finger next to her hand until it touched. She did not move away, so I felt more confident and put my hand on hers and said, "We'll be going ashore soon and perhaps never see each other again." She replied "I guess so." I took her hand and we went for a walk around the deck conversing about our future goals, in Russian. I became somewhat attached to her and didn't want this trip to end. She was perhaps the first girlfriend I ever had. I was becoming aware of my emotions at this time. We had a nice long walk and then she excused herself to be with her mother.

I also went below, and when my dad asked where I was all this time I told him of the Russian friend. We spent the rest of the evening talking about good manners and making nice impression on the people that might be meeting us at the dock. I became used to the canvas hammock that was my bed for the past week. I had a restful night swaying slightly with the motion of the ship. I enjoyed pleasant thoughts of my walking and talking with Sonia while holding her hand the day before.

In the morning, rumors began to circulate that we might be docking in New York that afternoon. I could hardly believe it! It was time to gather and pack our personal belongings, which consisted of one large and one small old piece of luggage held secured with leather belts because the locks did not work. We had with us nothing of value, only a small old Leica camera which we later sold. We used the money for food. I put on my best clothes, which weren't really much, and went topside to say goodbye to Sonia. I found her also dressed in her best apparel. Relatives were meeting her also. We spent an hour or so talking and finally I gathered enough courage to kiss her very gently on her lips. It seemed appropriate since we would never see each other again. She responded cautiously as she placed her right hand on the left side of my face and closed her eyes momentarily till the kiss ended. I turned around and walked toward the stairway and turned back to see if she was watching me. She had her head turned to the left and waved goodbye, smiling.

I went below, gathered my belongings, and went topside with Dad and his cousin. The deck became very crowded with people and luggage. Everyone wanted to be the first to see America. There was no way to get anywhere near the railing now. Suddenly someone shouted "The Statue of Liberty!" and everyone turned in its direction to see. It was a magnificent sight. Everyone's eyes were upon her until our ship passed; a most impressive structure. I doubt if anyone could have appreciated her more than we did at that time. We were approaching New York Harbor and our hearts began pounding at an ever—increasing rate. "America, America," people shouted. "We are here, we are here!" Tears of joy were visible on everyone's face as the Statue of Liberty grew alive with gentleness, welcoming us to this new free land!

A tugboat approached our ship and the harbor captain came aboard to guide us through the harbor. Not much time passed before we could see the New York skyline in the twilight with many brightly lit buildings silhouetted against the darkened sky. The harbor with all its docks was within our reach. We were taking bets which berth our ship would dock in. We saw people on the dock waving to us, an unbelievable sight. *WE HAD ARRIVED IN AMERICA, ON A NEW CONTINENT! REMARKABLE!*

One and a half years after arriving in America. I grew a lot. Father and I put on much needed weight.

Chapter 16

Arriving in America

More than anything, I wanted to jump ship and be the first to kiss the soil of this new land. I anxiously watched a sailor throw the ropes. The large motors began taking up the slack as the ship moved closer and closer to the dock until the water between ship and dock was no longer visible. We felt a sudden bang as the hull touched the wooden pilings and came to a complete halt.

Everyone was looking for friends and relatives. We were expecting someone from the Joint Organization to meet us, but we did not know who it might be. We didn't know who to look for. We took some paper, wrote our name on it and pinned it to our lapels in hope that someone would recognize our names. The gangway was lowered and people rushed to disembark. My main concern was to stay close to my dad. I didn't want to face the United States all by myself, not even knowing the language. Our turn came and we began to walk down the gangway. I was holding on to my dad's jacket, afraid of being separated.

We walked to a big building and inside were many people waiting for the new arrivals. I had sent a picture of myself to some people from the Grodner' Club. The members were people from Grodno who had immigrated to **America** before the war. One middle—aged man shouted to me as I passed,

"Hirshel!" I nodded my head, yes. He took me around and gave me a big hug. It was my mother's cousin, Jack Cohen, and his wife Helen. Soon a few others surrounded us, one was Herman Yablakoff, a Yiddish actor who performed for many years at the Yiddish theater in New York, wrote at least one book in Yiddish, and was very well known in Jewish circles.

Mr. and Mrs. Cohen had an automobile. We were ushered to the roomy rear seat and were taken to their apartment in Brooklyn. I had never been in an automobile before and I was amazed at all the gauges and controls on the dash. It was already getting dark and the illuminated instruments held my attention. We had arrived at the apartment and were guided to an elevator. The door closed and our cousin pushed the number 11 button. The elevator began to move. I was wondering what if it failed to stop and went all the way to the top. Would it turn over and go upside down? We had no elevators in Poland and I had nothing to compare it to. It was another first experience. The elevator stopped on the 11th floor as it was supposed to. The elevator door opened for us automatically and we found ourselves standing in a big, long hallway. The hallway extended about sixty feet in both directions. We turned right and walked to a door which displayed number 1127. Jack had the key ready in his hand and opened the door. Inside was the most beautiful, spacious apartment that I had ever seen. There was a large living room with a high ceiling. The floor was covered with Persian rugs; the furniture was old but good quality, in excellent condition. It had a grand view of Ocean Avenue in Brooklyn. There were at least two bedrooms, well furnished, and a large dining room filled with glossy cherry—wood furniture. The apartment was like a palace to me. Mrs. Cohen (Helen) watched my excitement build as I went from room to room observing and admiring everything in sight. They had no children of their own and I seem to have brought some joy into their lives. After washing up, we were served a very nice home—cooked meal which Helen had already prepared. It was elegantly served in the formal dining room. We spent the rest of the evening and late into the night answering questions about the war and about our missing relatives. Unfortunately, we had to tell them that to the best of our knowledge no one else had survived. Mrs. Cohen ushered us into our designated bedrooms, where we spent a very comfortable night.

In the morning, after a nice breakfast of juice, bagel and lox, scrambled eggs, and coffee, they made plans for us to go shopping for some new clothes. Our old European clothes were twenty years or so out of style and it must have been embarrassing for them to show us off the way we were dressed. My cousins took us on the subway to Manhattan. I was walking along Fifth Avenue with my head arched back and my eyes straight up watching for the very top of all the tall skyscrapers. First they took us into a ladies' store and bought a complete outfit for Lona and then to a men's store to purchase new clothes for Dad and me. Cousin Jack opened his wallet and I saw many one dollar bills. It looked like a great deal of money to me. He paid for our purchases in cash, of course. There were no credit cards available then, to the best of my knowledge. It felt so good being dressed in properly fitted clothes. Another first experience. After lunch in an automated cafeteria we went to visit their friends and others who might be interested in meeting us. Mr. Cohen owned a small hotel in Brooklyn and was able to devote a lot of time to us, for which we were very grateful. We accepted several invitations to other people's homes for dinner and conversation.

The next day, they took us again to New York to see the sights. We went to the Empire State Building, Radio City Music Hall, the Statue of Liberty, museums and many other places of interest.

While in a downtown restaurant ordering tea, I said to the waiter "Only a half glass, please." Mrs. Cohen said to me in Yiddish, "Why did you only order a half glass? You could order a full glass and drink only what you want." My reply to her was, "I did not want to waste the water." It was difficult for her to understand that I considered water to be so precious. I noticed at our table there were containers of sugar, salt, and pepper. I said to Mrs. Cohen, "Helen, doesn't anyone steal the sugar?" I think that she began to understand the situation. She explained to me that in this country this is how it is done. To have all the sugar I wanted for my tea was ecstasy. I realized that I had a lot more to learn besides English.

Everyone was nice to me and I was eager to show my gratefulness and appreciation. My cousins took a liking to me and asked me if I wanted to stay with them in Brooklyn. Dad and Lona encouraged me to stay. They continued, "We have nothing to offer you once we arrive in Los Angeles to live with Uncle Julius. Here you will have a nice apartment, your own bedroom, what else do you want?" Lona exclaimed. I began to feel that I was in the way and wasn't wanted. I could see that Lona wanted my dad to herself. Dad also said that I would be better off here. My heart became heavy with sorrow and I began to miss my mother desperately. I had no one to communicate my feelings to. I felt all alone in the world again.

Once again, I was faced with a major decision: Should I give up my dad and stay with the Cohens, or go with them to Los Angeles, knowing that they would rather I didn't? It was painful either way. I swallowed my pride and said to Dad, "I'd rather be with you no matter what my future will be. I have lost everyone else in my family. You are the only one I have left. I want to be with you!" That ended the conversation on that subject and we went to bed, exhausted. I informed the Cohens that I appreciated their generous offer but wanted to remain with Dad after going through so much together in the camps.

We spent a whole week in New York sightseeing and meeting new people who were interested in the whereabouts of their relatives. Most of our comments about the families in Europe were of a negative nature. Some of them gave us a few dollars, which was greatly appreciated. We already had our train tickets paid for with the money that we sent to Uncle Julius in Los Angeles. Mr. and Mrs. Cohen took us to Central Station, and after buying us a few goodies, put us on the train headed for the West Coast.

We quickly found our seats and waved through the window at the Cohens as our train began pulling out of the station. I noticed a tear roll down cousin Helen's face as she waved to us. I know that she was fond of me and wanted me to stay.

I was fascinated with the New York architecture and enjoyed the passing scenery as the train moved by the tall buildings and then the countryside. I felt the need to see every passing house, field, farm and hills. It was all new to me. The vastness of the entire continent lay before me. There was no better way to see it than by train and I did not want to miss a thing. Our friends had given us plenty of food to take on board and that saved our precious dollars which we so greatly treasured. We couldn't afford sleepers, so we made ourselves as comfortable as possible in our seats, to spend the next three days and nights on the train.

Riding the train to California was another great experience. This train was fast, smooth, clean, and had sparkling bathroom facilities. Above all, this train was taking us to a *new life* in Los Angeles, not to another death camp as was the case so often in the past. I didn't want to make constant comparisons with life in Germany. I guess it must have been natural to do so. I couldn't help it. I so desperately wanted to forget everything of the past. I was too young to know that it wasn't possible.

The three days and nights on the train passed quickly. I really enjoyed the surge of new information about the vastness and beauty of this great land which I had been absorbing all day. Our train was about to approach the outskirts of Los Angeles. We had telephoned Uncle Julius from New York about our arrival schedule. He said he would meet us at the train station. We anxiously looked forward to meeting him and his family with whom we'd be staying. The tracks were numerous as our train slowly inched toward the L.A. train depot. It was time to again gather our personal belongings and get ready to disembark. The train came to a halt and the conductor shouted, "Los Angeles, everyone out." A shock wave went up my spine with the realization that we had actually arrived at a place we so often talked about in a distant land. We had sent Uncle Julius recent photographs for identification. As we disembarked, he and Aunt Lakie came over to me and shouted "Hirshel!" I responded, "Yes." She gave me a big hug and so did Uncle Julius, and they took us to their automobile.

The car was a 1936 Chevrolet four—door, in clean, cared—for condition. The three of us got into the back seat and our luggage was put in the trunk. Uncle Julius was a tailor, a man of modest means and a big heart. The hour ride to his home in west Los Angeles was very pleasant. We answered many questions about our trip and how we liked America. We pulled up to a little corner house near W. Adams & La Brea. Uncle Julius said, "This is it." He pulled into his little one—car driveway, which was lined with two strips of concrete with grass growing in between. We got out of the car. They had two sons who came out to greet us. I was delighted to meet my cousins, whom I was most anxious to befriend. They would be my first pals and would certainly help me with English and familiarize me with American customs.

We walked inside. The house must have been no more than 700 square feet. It consisted of a living room, a kitchen with breakfast nook, one small bathroom, and two small bedrooms. Uncle Julius and Aunt Lakie occupied one bedroom, their two sons the other. Dad and his cousin could sleep on the couch. For me, Uncle Julius enclosed half of his front porch. It gave me a room approximately four feet by six feet. There was enough room for one six—foot bunk, a one-foot walking space, and a one—by—three foot cabinet. I was very grateful for the accommodations. It was more than I ever had before. Aunt Lakie did the cooking for all of us. We were to stay there until Dad could find a job and get settled.

A week later, Dad asked Julius if there was anything left over from the money that we sent him from Germany after deducting for our passage to New York and train fare to Los Angeles. His reply was, "There are a few hundred dollars remaining. You can stay here for awhile and that remaining money will take care of your room and board." It was painful, but we had no choice. With no jobs yet and not speaking the language, there was nowhere else for us to go.

My cousins turned out to be a disappointment to me. When I asked questions, they considered me inferior for not being as knowledgeable as they were. They advised me to find the answers in books, knowing that I couldn't read English. They did not introduce me to any of their friends as I hoped they would. I could see clearly that I would have to make friends alone, the hard way. I immediately enrolled in a high school that offered English classes to new immigrants. At the end of the first semester, I knew enough English to begin regular school. I enrolled in the neighborhood high school and was determined to get my high school diploma.

In the meantime, Uncle Julius got Dad and Lona a job at the garment factory where he worked. Dad worked as a presser and Lona as a seamstress. I found a weekend job at a local bakery. Dad and Lona were accumulating money, and when a small one-bedroom apartment next door became vacant, they rented it for $32.00 a month and decided to get married. I moved in with them. Lona suggested that I also pay some money for room and board. I barely had enough money for school supplies and lunch money and an occasional movie. Dad gave me a few dollars every month on the side without Lona's knowledge and instructed me to pay her to keep peace in the family.

They had a small wedding for some of their new friends. Dad invited me to the wedding. I told him that I couldn't go. I couldn't bear someone else taking the place of my mother just yet; I thought that she and my brother might still be alive. I went to a movie by myself to pass the time. I cried the whole time and it wasn't because of the picture.

In the new apartment, Dad and Lona had the bedroom and I slept on the couch in the 10' x 10' foot square living room. I wanted to finish high school as soon as possible because I was already seventeen years old. I spoke with my high school counselor and she arranged for me to take algebra One and algebra Two in one class. I did the homework for both and received double the credits. I did the same thing in summer school.

I made several new friends in high school and began to attend school parties and functions. I was arranging dates for my cousin because he had access to his father's car, which provided transportation as long as we were double dating.

Speaking the language enabled me to get a second job working for a drug store as a stock boy. My hours were long, from 4:30 p.m. to 10:00 p.m., sometimes longer, five days a week. It took me an hour on the bus to get to work. I used that time to complete my homework. After one year, and going to summer school for two summers, I finally completed high school and graduated at age 18. No one had the time to come to my graduation. I felt as if I were the only student there without parents. I had to make excuses why Dad didn't attend. I told my friends that he was ill.

I wasn't to be denied my graduation party. I asked my dad if I could have a small party at the apartment for my friends in honor of my graduation. After discussing it with Lona they reluctantly agreed. I asked them if they would mind going to a movie that evening or visit friends so we could have the space for ourselves. They agreed to that request also. The apartment was very small, as I mentioned earlier—the living room was no more that 10' x 10'. It contained a sofa, an easy chair, and a couple of coffee tables and a floor lamp. There was no room to stand. After my folks left, I invited a couple of my best friends to come over before the party was to begin. We took out all the furniture, including the large carpet that was covering the hardwood floor, and put it all in the backyard. That left a good-sized dance floor. I purchased soft drinks and chips. One of the girls I knew brought some onion dip. I had a phonograph and friends brought records and we all had a good, clean time. I must have had at least 50 kids there. We did make a little too much noise and a neighbor called the police. Dad and Lona returned a little earlier than expected and found a house full of kids, the police on the scene, and all the living room furniture gone. By the expressions on their faces, I thought for sure that they would make me move out the very next day. The party broke up quickly after that, and a couple of my friends stayed to help me restore the carpet and the furniture to the living room. They also helped me clean the place up. Fortunately, there was no damage to the apartment or to any of the furnishings. I was warned that I could not have any more parties there.

Right after graduation, I was beginning to be pressured to get married. Dad and Lona informed me that many of my friends were getting married at 18. I wanted to go to college, but no support or encouragement was offered. I had too little money to go out on my own. The money that we saved in Germany, which belonged to the three of us, became theirs only; I was excluded. As an alternate choice, I wanted to go into business for myself. I was a qualified mechanic and had also completed machinist school in Germany after the war. The little money I called my own wasn't enough to pay the rent and utilities. I needed to buy machine tools and the cost was prohibitive.

Uncle Julius was very nice to me and wanted to help. He and Aunt Lakie saw the situation that I was in and were sympathetic. I liked Julius and always helped him with anything that he needed. He was a "do—it—yourselfer" and I learned a lot by helping him. He would say to me, "Harold, will you please help me do the lawn?" I always helped eagerly. Aunt Lakie was a very good—natured person and was like a mother to me. Often she would say, "Harold, will you be kind enough to go to the store for me? I forgot to get this and that." I never said no to her. I was eager to help in any way that I could to demonstrate my appreciation.

There was a gentleman in his seventies who used to come with his wife to visit the family. His name was Sam Berman. He was retired from the garment industry. His wife Eva was Aunt Lakie's sister. They used to visit a lot and Eva liked to play cards with Lakie. Sam didn't have much to do while he was waiting, so he and I got into some interesting conversations and became very good friends. He took a strong liking to me. He noticed a special quality in me that he admired and he taught me the ways of this land. Sam coached me in etiquette and proper behavior. He was sensitive and noticed my lack of knowledge in American customs. He knew that it was of lack of education caused by my imprisonment in concentration camps for the past five years. He listened to my problems attentively and offered constructive advice. He and his wife had no children of their own.

On many occasions, Sam would say to me, "Harold, I know a very nice young lady who will be visiting here from Chicago. She comes from a very nice Jewish family and I think you ought to meet her." I said to Sam, "How old is she?" "Almost fourteen," he replied. "She is just a baby, much too young for me," I was past eighteen at that time. Sam continued in his soft, easygoing manner. "She is very mature for her age; you'll see." Every time he'd come over, the conversation always led to this very pretty, nice, young lady who would be visiting soon. We'd do all of our talking in his shining black Pontiac that was parked in front of our apartment. We had our privacy; besides, there was more room in his car than in our apartment!

The day finally arrived when the Schoenburg family came to visit. I came home from work and walked into Uncle Julius's house for something, and there in the kitchen nook was the most beautiful young lady: Soft blond hair, sky blue eyes and the warmest smile imaginable. Aunt Lakie said to me, "Harold, this is Joyce from Chicago." I replied, "Hello." I knew some English, but not enough to feel comfortable. I observed something in her that was very special as she sat there perfectly composed in her white Coca Cola dress. Her dress had lots of Coke bottles printed on it and that is why I called it the Coca Cola dress. She was very mature for her age, both physically and mentally. She and her family stayed for dinner and were to spend the evening there. I also had the pleasure of meeting her parents and younger sister Claire, who was five years her junior. I excused myself saying that I had much to do, but actually I didn't know how to converse in English.

Later that evening I returned to Uncle Julius's house after restoring my confidence somewhat. I spoke to Joyce's mother, Esther, in Yiddish, and she translated my words to Joyce in English: Very awkward, to say the least. I felt that her family liked me, but I wasn't sure whether it was because I was a novelty from a foreign country with interesting stories to tell, or if it was me personally, whom they liked. After conversing with Esther for awhile, I felt more comfortable asking her if I could take her daughter for a walk around the block. She replied, "I'll ask her." I saw Joyce nodding her head in a positive manner and I knew that the answer was yes. Her mother, her sister Claire and Aunt Lakie also came along and walked about three steps behind us. It was a beautiful warm evening and the walk was very pleasurable to me. Any questions I asked for the purpose of conversation were directed to her mother, who translated it to Joyce. She also had to go through her mother to ask me questions for further translation. After twice around the block, I asked Esther if I could hold Joyce's hand. After some translation, the answer was again affirmative. We laugh about it to this day as I tell this story to friends.

I asked Joyce for a date for the very next day because her family was returning to Chicago in just a few days. We took the bus to Westlake Park, rented a boat for an hour, and then went to the movies. It was a very pleasant afternoon for us both.

Shortly thereafter, Joyce and her family had to return to Chicago. We exchanged addresses before she left and I promised to write to her. She agreed to correspond. As my vocabulary increased, I was able to express myself more effectively. As a help to me, Joyce would include in her reply my original letter with corrected spelling. She was a very good speller and I learned much from her during the time we corresponded.

One day after Uncle Julius came home from work, and after we had supper, he said to me, "Harold, do you want to go with me? I want to help you find a job." "Yes, that would be great." I replied. He took me in his car to the gas station where he traded and introduced me to the owner. He said to the owner, "Jack, this is my nephew Harold, he is a mechanic. He is a refugee from Poland and a very nice boy. Can you give him a job?" Jack replied, "I can't give him a job, but I will sell him the gasoline and lube bay, part of the business. My partner and I will do the repairs and help him along." I got so excited! I thought to myself, what an opportunity to go into business on my own! Julius asked Jack, "How much will it cost?" "Two thousand dollars," he replied. "One thousand for the inventory and one thousand for good will." We told him we would think about it and get back to him in a day or so. That evening I discussed it with my dad. I had one thousand dollars saved up from working at the drug store for a year and a half while going to high school. Dad said that he would co—sign for a loan at the bank for the other thousand dollars. The next day we went to the bank and got the loan. The following afternoon the three of us—Dad, Uncle Julius, and I—went to the gas station and said to Jack, "We have the money you asked for, let's make a deal!"

Jack took a pad of note paper from his office and wrote out the agreement in longhand on one sheet of paper. I gave him the $2,000.00 check and Jack said to us, "You can take it over in the morning." The next morning, I arrived before seven and we took inventory. I put some change in the cash box and began to sell gasoline. It was so exciting being in my own business. Jack and his partner were very helpful at first, introducing me to all their regular customers. I worked the service station by myself in order to make enough money to pay off my $1,000.00 loan. I was doing all right and making regular payments to the bank as promised. Occasionally, I had to leave the station for a few minutes to get parts. Jack was always happy to watch the gas islands for me. He had a key to the cash box and I trusted him. He was like a father figure to me, teaching me the ropes, so to speak. One day I found out that while I was away getting parts, he had put some of the gasoline money in his pocket instead of in the register. I was very hurt and disappointed—not just because of the money but because I considered him a friend and advisor. I felt betrayed. From that point on I could no longer leave the station, and as a result, business suffered some. Parts stores did not have delivery service in those days.

Life at home was very unpleasant, knowing that Lona wanted me out of the house. Her motive was clear, she wanted Dad all to herself and I was like a bone in her throat. She would not allow me to even borrow my dad's tie for a special occasion, and also prohibited Dad from giving me gifts of any sort, even birthday gifts. If Dad gave me one of his used shirts, she'd take it away saying, "I gave it to your father for a gift and want only him to wear it." I began to envy young people who had their real mothers. I wondered why I had to be deprived of mine. She insisted that I pay room and board. I gave her what she asked so she would not upset my dad too much. When televisions were still rare in the year 1950, I bought a television for her as a gift in order to appease her. A few months later, as business improved, I bought her the latest Bendix automatic washing machine, also a novelty at that time. I believe that she was the only one in the neighborhood who possessed both a television and washing machine. No matter what I did, it was never quite right. She just wanted me to leave home.

I continued progressing in my business, paid off half of the bank loan that my dad had co—signed for, and even saved a nice amount. I expanded my circle of friends and was well accepted. My English also improved considerably. I was still paying off my debts and trying to save some money for a car. I wanted to have some money in my savings account before leaving home.

Although I was dating other Jewish girls, my interest in Joyce persisted, even though she lived so far away. Her intelligent letters and descriptions of life with her family were feelings that I longed for, not having a real family of my own. I wished that I could have a nice family also. In one of my letters, I wrote to her saying that I'd like to come and visit her that summer in Chicago. She replied that she had consulted with her parents and that I would be welcomed in her home. I answered that I was delighted and would be coming soon and could stay about two weeks.

I looked in the newspaper under "situations wanted", and found an ad advertising for a driver to share expenses to Chicago. I arranged to be the fourth driver and in a few days we were on the road. I had barely gotten my driver's license and not having a car of my own, I lacked the driving experience necessary for long—distance driving. There were no freeways at that time and most of the road to Chicago was two lanes with a white stripe down the center. Never having driven out of town before, I thought that the center line was to line up with the center of the hood ornament. I drove that way for many miles, scaring the occupants of the car to death. When a car approached from the opposite direction, I'd move over to the right of the road, and after we passed each other, I again returned to the center of the road as I thought I was supposed to. I obviously had a lot to learn about driving a car. . .

Three days later we arrived in Chicago. We pulled into a service station for gas and I called Joyce to tell her that I had arrived. When I called her home, she informed me that they were just on the way out of town for her uncle's wedding. Her father agreed to stop and pick me up along the way. They arrived within half an hour and included me in their party to the wedding.

I spent much time talking to Joyce and to her parents, who were very interested in my past. I'd help her mother with the dishes and the gardening in the back yard. I enjoyed spending time with Joyce's family. They were all very hospitable and made my vacation as pleasant as possible.

I returned to Los Angeles and continued with my work, evening education, and dating other girls. A few months had passed and my aunt received a call from Esther, Joyce's mother, saying that they were in Los Angeles because Joyce's grandfather had died. They would be staying for a few days. I called Joyce, asking if I could see her that evening. She replied that she would not go out but that I was welcome to visit with her family. I respected her decision not to go out and was very impressed with her morality. I felt that any girl that felt so strongly about her honor and about religious values was rare, and I became determined that she was to become my wife. I visited her the following evening.

Just as things were improving for me in business, the Korean War broke out. I was just the right age for the draft, although I was not yet an American Citizen. I was suddenly faced with the heavy problem of disposing of my business. There was a kosher butcher shop located across the street from my service station. Two brothers were the proprietors and were customers of mine. They weren't getting along too well and one of them approached me about selling the gas station to him. I agreed to sell for the same price that I paid for it one year earlier. The butcher didn't have enough money, so I had to take back a $500.00 note.

Joyce's father, Jim Schoenburg, took a new job as a produce sales manager in Salinas, in central California, only 17 miles from Fort Ord, and she and her entire family—mother, father, and sister Claire—moved there.

I joined the Army to serve my new country. I was grateful for the opportunity to have had my education and my own business. I reported to the Presidio in San Francisco for induction and was sent to Fort Ord for my basic training. Joyce and her family were already living in Salinas.

I had not yet become a U.S. citizen. I wore my Army uniform with great pride and satisfaction. The weeks of basic training that followed were difficult and demanding. No passes were permitted until the six—week training course was over. Often when out with my company on night maneuvers, I could clearly see the illuminated sky over Salinas, just a few miles away, where Joyce lived. I wished I could be with her instead of in the brush among the rattlesnakes and poison oak.

One morning very early, our company went into the brush for compass and map—reading courses. We marched for several miles to a designated area. There were bleachers for seating, and an instructor awaited us with an easel that had on it the display of the material we were about to learn. We were all dressed in full combat gear. We wore our steel helmets, fatigues, combat boots and fully loaded backpack. On our belts, we carried with us a canteen, ammunition, and bayonet on the right sides of our bodies. We were ordered to remove our backpacks, to place our M—1 rifles in stacks and to occupy the bleachers—all at double time. I was a little slow removing my backpack because of a sunburn I had gotten a few days before when I had my shirt off for too long a time. By the time I got to the bleachers, all the seats were taken and I had to sit on the ground to the right of the bleachers where others who couldn't find a place were sitting.

We were approximately half an hour into the training program when someone shouted, "I hear a rattlesnake!" I turned my head to the right, and six feet in that direction I saw a coiled up rattlesnake, about six feet long and two and a half inches in diameter, rattling his tail. By that time, everyone became aware of the situation, including the instructor. I don't know what prompted me to do it other than keen instinct, but I reached for my bayonet and removed it from the holder. I picked up the bayonet by the tip with my right hand and threw it at the head of the snake. The bayonet spun several times in mid-air. Its point pierced the neck of the snake just below the head and pinned it to the ground. With disbelief, everyone watched with amazement as I went over, grabbed the bayonet by the handle, and pulled it out of the ground with the rattlesnake still dangling from it. One of my soldier friends took photographs that I treasure to this day. I became an instant hero and this story circulated in my battalion for a long time.

I have attempted many times since then to duplicate my knife—throwing technique but without success. I never threw a knife successfully before or ever again. It must have been some of my remaining luck left over from Germany.

After six weeks of basic training, I was allowed weekend passes. What a joy it was to spend weekends with Joyce and her loving family! We fell deeply in love and were planning to be married. My stay at Fort Ord did not last long. We got deeper into the war and more troops were sent to Korea daily.

My (MOS) Military Occupational Specialty was machinist and mechanic. I was assigned to an ordnance company. A mobile machine shop became my home, so to speak. I worked in a thirty—foot semi truck which was a completely equipped machine shop. We had a lathe, drill press, shaper, milling machine, work benches, grinders, and all the hand tools imaginable. We also had a complete inventory of metal stock, an electric welder, and a self—contained generator to power our shop. We often moved to various locations and repaired broken parts and made new ones.

I thought I was lucky when I was sent to build Camp Irwin near Barstow, California. I suppose I was. The alternative was to be sent to Korea. After returning from five years in Germany, Korea was the last place on earth that I wanted to be. Camp Irwin was, I believe, an armored vehicle training base. My company was sent there to maintain and repair tanks and support vehicles. The nights were very cold and the days hot. It was difficult to perform maintenance out in the open with the wind constantly blowing sand into the exposed transmission parts and into our faces. Although I was not far from Salinas, getting a three—day pass was very difficult. About every other month, I somehow managed to get a three—day pass and come home.

I received a notice from the Monterey County Courthouse to appear and be sworn in as a United States citizen. I was jumping with joy. Armed with this letter, I went to my company commander requesting a pass for this all—important occasion. The company commander reacted favorably and issued me a three—day pass along with his congratulations.

One of my friends who was also from Salinas said to me, "I hear that you'll be going to Salinas soon to become a citizen. I have a car parked at a Barstow service station. Would you like to pick it up and take it to my home? I don't need it here and it will serve as one—way transportation for you." I was delighted and thanked him profusely for his kind offer. He gave me the keys to his car and told me where it was parked.

Late one evening, when it was time for me to take the trip I caught a ride to Barstow in an Army vehicle and was taken to the small service station where this car was stored. It was an old Mercury. I can't recall the model year. I inserted the key into the door lock and the lock didn't work. I went around to the passenger side and managed to get it unlocked. I slid over to the driver's side behind the wheel and tried to familiarize myself with all the instruments. The car was parked on a slight embankment facing downhill. I put the key in the ignition, released the emergency brake and stepped on the brake pedal. The brake pedal went all the way to the floor and the car began to roll. I quickly put the shift lever in gear, pulled on the hand operated emergency brake and managed to bring the vehicle to a halt. The floor board was missing in the front passenger compartment so the master cylinder was clearly exposed at my feet. I found a pair of pliers, managed to undo the nut, and discovered that all the brake fluid had leaked out of the master cylinder. It was already 10:00 p.m. and I had to be in Salinas in the morning for my naturalization ceremony. I couldn't miss that at any cost.

I figured that I could drive with only the emergency brake. It would be night driving and there would be very light traffic on the road. I turned the ignition key to start and nothing happened. I looked at the dash and noticed a starting button. When I touched it the engine began to crank. However, there was not enough electrical power in the battery to get it started. Automotive was my specialty, so I did not give up yet. I turned the ignition key to on, put the floor transmission lever in second gear and very carefully released the emergency brake while depressing the clutch pedal. The car began to roll forward and after it picked up sufficient speed I released the clutch pedal and got it started. What a relief it was to hear the engine operating. I was on my way! As I looked down at the floorboard, I could see the road passing underneath my feet. Every time the wheels hit a puddle on the road my legs were splashed with water. It was cold and the heater didn't work.

I reached Tehachapi Pass, which I knew would be the toughest part of this trip. Once beyond the pass, the rest of the trip would be easy. As I approached the pass it began to snow. I tried the windshield wipers and they, also, were inoperative. I had to keep the windows open to look for the white line on the road while the slush splashing in through the floor board was solidifying around the bottom of my legs. In my mind I kept saying, "What did I get myself into? One slip and this old car would go over the side of the road and down the ravine, and I will never be found." I kept thinking, "What if the engine dies? I will never be able to get it restarted uphill."

Much snow had already accumulated on the road as I was approaching the summit. The road became icy and very slippery. I kept the car in second gear and was advancing slowly. Every once in a while, the wheels would begin to spin and the car would slide backwards down the road. That was the most scary part. I had the driver's door slightly ajar so that I could jump out in the event the car went over the side.

I reached the summit safely and was beginning to go downhill. What a relief it was! I still kept it in second gear. I did not have a foot brake and I had no idea how long the emergency brake would work. Everything was going well. I came down the mountain safely and was thinking how I would approach my friend who was kind enough to lend me this wreck of a car. My legs were still frozen with the slush and I was bitter cold. I knew that soon I would be driving on a long stretch of level road. There was no radio in the car and I kept my mind occupied thinking about the various things I'd be doing after getting home. Up until this moment, most of my concentration was directed to keeping this vehicle safely on the road. I was beginning to relax somewhat, knowing that the most difficult part of the trip was already behind me and in three more hours, I would be home.

I crossed the beautiful San Joaquin Valley and was enjoying the smell of the fields. The temperature became a bit warmer and my pants thawed out. I would look down through the floorboard occasionally and watch the dry, dusty air entering the vehicle through the floor. I was thinking what a story I could tell about this trip when I reached home. I had no idea that the worst part of my trip still lay ahead.

I was approaching Paso Robles. Scattered houses appeared on both sides of the road, and illuminated motel and restaurant signs indicated that the city was just a few miles away. It was about 1:00 a.m. I figured that I would be home by 3:00 a.m. and would be able to get a few hours of needed sleep before appearing in court for my citizenship papers.

I reached Paso Robles and was about to cross the railroad tracks, which were right out of town. As I approached the tracks, the engine died. I tried restarting it without success. I opened the door, stepped out, and lifted the hood to look for possible problems.

I suddenly heard a train whistle in the distance and became concerned about the approaching train. My car was stalled in the middle of both tracks. I quickly closed the hood and tried to push the car off the track. It wouldn't move. I realized that I left it in gear because the emergency brake did not hold too well. I rushed over to open the driver's door. The door handle did not work and the window was closed. I could see the rotating headlight of the locomotive approaching at great speed. Being very concerned about the safety of the borrowed car, I became determined to save it at all costs. I ran over to the passenger side, opened the door and pushed the gear shift lever into neutral.

As I closed the door, the locomotive was coming around the bend and was in plain view, just a few hundred feet from the crossing. The whistle blew very loud once more and I ran toward the back of the vehicle. I turned my back toward the car, grabbed the rear bumper with both hands and began pushing. The tracks were level and the car was light so it began moving immediately. I dug my heels into the pavement and pushed against the rear of the car with my back, using all my strength. The train engineer obviously did not see the situation and was advancing at normal speed. After I pushed the car off the track, the road went slightly uphill, making pushing harder. The locomotive was at the crossing and my legs were still near the tracks. I braced my legs against the end of the railroad ties and leaned back at a 45°angle. I stiffened my legs and saw the train pass before my eyes as a blur. My knees were only inches away underneath the passing box cars. I felt my legs weakening while the weight of the vehicle was pushing against me. It was a long train and the end was nowhere in sight. I kept praying that my knees would hold until the train passed. Suddenly there were no more railroad cars before my eyes and I relaxed my grip from around the rear bumper.

I stood there motionless and watched the car roll back onto the railroad track. I sat on the rear bumper for a few minutes trying to compose myself. The train sped away in the darkness, completely unaware of the near accident. There was total silence, as if nothing ever happened. I opened the car door and turned the key in the ignition and tried starting once more. The motor started instantly and I slowly drove into town, found the nearest coffee shop and sat down in a booth, calming my nerves with a cup of black coffee.

The rest of the trip to Salinas was uneventful, but I could not drive safely above 50 mph. My nerves did not recover as quickly as I had hoped. I made it home safely, told my story to Joyce (who had become my wife several months before) and made it to the courthouse on time to receive my citizenship papers. This event was one of the happiest in my life. I was very proud to become an American citizen.

I returned to Barstow by bus. After arriving at camp, I related this eventful trip to the friend who had lent me his car. I thought that he would be grateful to me for risking my life to save his automobile from the train. Instead he replied, "I wish you'd left it on the tracks. The car wasn't worth much."

I remained in Camp Irwin for a few more months after I became a U.S. citizen. Immediately thereafter, we shipped out to another camp in Nevada where some top secret experiments were being performed and another *great danger awaited me!*

Chapter 17

Atomic Explosions at Desert Rock, Nevada

Desert Rock, Nevada, located some fifty or so miles north of Las Vegas, was the next Army base that I was transferred to. I was again assigned to an ordinance company there. I was glad to remain in the United States. Going to Korea after recently returning from five years of war and Nazi imprisonment wasn't exactly what I needed at that time. I had no way of knowing that I would be among those troops to be used in experiments with radiation tests of the atom bomb.

After arriving at Desert Rock, our ordinance company spent many weeks building and repairing equipment. Even though we were close to Las Vegas, we seldom got a chance to go there. I spent much of my spare time cutting hair and earning a little extra money to send home to supplement my $90.00 a month salary.

One evening, we were told that the next morning at 4:00 a.m. we were to dress in full combat uniforms and assemble in front of our barracks for maneuvers. We wore our fatigues and helmets and carried our M—1 rifles with bayonets on our belts. Several trucks arrived to pick us up. We were taken out into the desert. There we joined other soldiers who had arrived earlier, and the rumor circulated that we were about to witness an *"Atomic Explosion."* A voice was heard over the many loudspeakers that were installed high on tripods. "Good morning soldiers. You are about to witness an atomic explosion. You are located approximately six miles from Ground Zero, where you are safe. We will give each of you a film strip which you will wear on your lapel to measure the radiation, if any, that you might be exposed to. Also a pair of dark glasses so that you can look at the explosion after the initial blast." We were told that we stood at a safe distance and not to be concerned, or words to that effect.

The first beam of sun rays appeared in the eastern horizon. The voice over the loudspeakers began giving information and instructions. "Six minutes from blast." Some of my friends looked up high in the sky and shouted, "I can see the plane," and others looked in the same direction. Finally I, also, was able to see a shiny moving dot, streaking across the sky. It was the B—29 that was to drop the atom-bomb. "Ground Zero" was pointed out to us. It was the spot in the desert where the A—bomb was supposed to land. Six miles in the vastness of the desert wasn't very far. We could all see that spot very clearly. What if it misses the target by a few miles, in our direction? What then? I thought. The voice over the loudspeaker interrupted my thoughts: "Four minutes to zero; if you look up to the sky at 12 o'clock you can see the plane." I continued to memorize the landscape as it was before the blast, to compare it after detonation, that is, if we were still alive. "Two minutes from zero. You are to put on your protective dark eye glasses and turn around 180 degrees so that your back is facing Ground Zero." We all obeyed orders and turned around awaiting the inevitable.

"You are not to turn around," the voice continued, "Until you see a flash of bright light followed by a blast. A strong wind will also occur. When you feel the wind kneel to the ground." There was silence. None of us had ever experienced this previously. W e wondered if we should have written home the day before. "The bomb is on its way. Touchdown will occur in two minutes," or words to that effect were heard over the loudspeaker. It was difficult to comprehend that the A—bomb was released from the plane, us knowing about it and not feeling the pain. These were two of the longest minutes I can remember. In utter silence, we were awaiting a huge explosion. The voice continued, "One minute till zero; I will cease counting 15 seconds before blast." The tension and the uncertainty of the situation kept building within us, anticipation of the blast of unknown proportions and its effect on us. "50 seconds, 40 seconds, 30 seconds." We could bear it no longer as we stood there in a kneeling position with our backs to Ground Zero, waiting for it to happen. There was a sudden silence as the announcer failed to give us further information.

Suddenly there was a bright flash of light reflecting from the nearby mountains. I felt a flash of heat at the back of my neck, between jacket and helmet, the only part of my skin that was exposed. Then there was silence. Some seconds later, I don't recall how many, there was a loud blast of thunder that shook the countryside. We all turned around and saw the actual ball of fire rising into the sky. The voice on the loudspeaker could be heard again. "The mushroom cloud has risen to twenty thousand feet."

251

It was huge, it was red, it was violent. "Forty thousand feet," the voice continued. A strong wind, hurricane force, swept down upon us, bringing with it dust, sand, and flying objects torn loose along the way. It lasted for 10 to 15 seconds, then it was over. We recovered, shook the dust off our clothes and made small talk about the event that had just occurred. We were actually glad to be alive, without any visible damage to ourselves. We were beginning to relax when suddenly and without prior warning from the announcer, we were again hit by a strong wind returning from the nearby mountains and heading back to the direction of the explosion, again bringing with it large amounts of dust. In minutes, the dust was sucked up into the atmosphere and the sky darkened above us. We were ordered to return the strips of film that we wore on our lapels to measure the amount of radiation we were exposed to. We boarded the waiting trucks and returned to our tents. For several days after the blast I had sunburn on the back of my neck, on the small part of my skin that was unprotected and exposed.

That was not the last time I witnessed an atomic explosion at Desert Rock. There were several more explosions similar in scope. The second time we knew what to expect. The tension was not as intense, but the danger of being exposed to radiation was awesome.

In addition to my regular duties on base, I cut hair for my battalion in the off—duty hours. My skills were needed and the $0.50 per haircut amounted to a sizable sum. I even cut the company commander's hair on many occasions.

In the summer, the heat in the desert was unbearable, way over 100°, and in the winter the nights were freezing cold. We still lived in canvas tents with a wooden floor. The days were long and the weeks dragged on. I had been there more than a year now and was missing my new wife and the stability of a home of my own which I had always longed for. On occasion, between tests, I'd sometimes be able to arrange for a three—day pass to go home and visit Joyce and our family. The distance to Salinas was about 500 miles. By bus it would take almost 24 hours. I'd do it anyway. It would at least give me one day with my wife.

Once I got a ride from Desert Rock to Nellis Air Force base, near Las Vegas. Occasionally a soldier could hitch a ride on an Air Force plane if space was available. After checking with the tower, I was informed that there would be a B—29 going to Travis Air Force Base, near San Francisco, in a few hours. The flight wouldn't take more than a couple of hours and would place me less than two hundred miles from my destination, thus allowing me to spend that much more time with my wife and her family. I was delighted. I was introduced to the crew and was told that first I must check out a parachute. Those were the regulations. Any additional personnel flying in Air Force planes had to have a chute. I went to supply and one was issued to me. I boarded the big plane and in minutes we were airborne. I asked the pilot if I could sit in the lower turret for greater visibility. He very graciously allowed me to do so, seeing how interested I was. I was told that we'd make a short stop in Reno, only for a couple of minutes or so, and then nonstop to Travis.

We landed in Reno. The engines didn't even stop and we were on our way again in minutes. As soon as we reached cruising altitude, I noticed that we were being attacked by two jet fighters. I could see their tracer bullets heading toward us from the north, the right side of the plane. I tried to contact the crew on the intercom. The intercom in my turret must have been disconnected or was inoperative. They were getting ready to make another pass at us—I could see them circling. I rushed out of the turret as quickly as my legs would allow and headed toward the cockpit to inform the crew. When I arrived there breathless, and after I managed to say what I was trying to tell them, the captain replied, "Oh, we forgot to tell you. We stopped at Reno to pick up a tow target. They were our jets target practicing. We'll be dropping the target in a couple of minutes." What a relief!

Our plane landed safely at Travis and in a short couple of hours I arrived in Salinas, where my wife's father, Jim, met me at the bus station and drove me home. We were all happy to see each other. The precious hours with my wife passed quickly. There were no flights going to Nellis Air Force Base and I had to take a Greyhound back to Las Vegas. I would have to take the 12:00 midnight bus to make it in time for Monday morning reveille at Desert Rock. In the evening, after a fun—filled day and after my in—laws went to bed, my wife's younger sister Claire, my wife, and I sat down on the floor in front of the fireplace to talk. We all fell asleep. Suddenly, like an alarm clock, Joyce woke up five minutes before twelve and shouted. "Harold! Hurry, you are going to miss your bus." I quickly put on my jacket while she called a cab and her sister handed me the parachute (the one I checked out previously at Nellis, and carried with me on the bus all the way from San Francisco). By the time I kissed Joyce goodbye, the cab was waiting outside the door. I threw the parachute in the back seat and told the driver to please hurry to the bus station, which was only a few blocks away.

We arrived at the bus station just as the bus was leaving. I jumped out of the cab and chased after the bus while shouting for it to stop and banging on its side with my fist. Luckily, the driver heard me, stopped the bus, and opened the front door. I was out of breath. I threw the parachute inside the bus, next to the driver's seat, and climbed into the bus myself. The driver swiftly closed the pneumatic door and picked up the parachute by the handle to move it out of my way. The chute popped open and in seconds it was all over the bus. I spent the rest of the night folding the chute without success.

The next day I called home to tell Joyce how narrowly I made it. She replied, "I know. I called the bus station because I was worried. I asked the dispatcher if he saw a soldier in uniform take the bus to Vegas, and I began to describe you. He stopped me and said, 'you mean the one with the parachute.' I said 'Yes.' 'He made it all right' and went on to tell me the story about the open chute." We still laugh about it to this day.

I had enough of war and weapons. I counted each day, waiting for the time I could return home for good and build a new, free life with my wife.

This photo of me with my Company was taken at Fort Ord, when I graduated from basic—training about March 1951.

Chapter 18

Unfinished Commitments

I had only one more month remaining to serve in the armed forces. My two—year tour of duty was almost over and orders came through for me to be transferred to Camp Roberts in California. The last month at Camp Roberts was a scorcher, with temperatures of over 100° daily. In the middle of January 1953, I was handed an honorable discharge and finally went home to Salinas.

The period of my life from the end of the Korean War until the present has been very good for me. I built a home for my family using the California Veterans benefits—a very low interest loan which is now paid off. After spending a few years in the produce business with my wife's family, I decided to do the things I knew best. I purchased a service station and have been with the same company for more than 36 years.

I had a list of a few things that I had to with my life before it was over.

1. I had to find Berl Lom and convince him that I did not steal his bread ration in the concentration camp. I discovered that he remarried and also emigrated to the United States and was operating an army surplus store in New Orleans, Louisiana. I called him on the phone and informed him that I was in Texas working on a farm and would like to visit him on Passover. He was delighted that I called and he invited me for the Passover Seder.

I arrived at his home a week later. He and his wife were very cordial and hospitable to me. They had several of their friends over for a traditional Passover meal. We all sat down to eat at a beautiful dining room table decorated with a lace tablecloth, and all the traditional dishes were served. The service was about to begin and the wine was being poured. I said to Berl, "Berl, there is something I must say to you now before we start. Can I have a few moments?" He replied, "Yes, of course." I said, "Berl, I have to tell you something here before your friends and before God. *I did not steal your bread ration in the concentration camp!*" He replied, "Who cares, it was so long ago." I said "No, it matters to me that you believe me. *I did not take it!*" We put our arms around each other and he realized that I meant what I said. I felt satisfied and left for home the following day.

2.   The second thing I needed to do, was to find out if Mr. Wise, the jeweler from the Grodno ghetto to whom we returned the gold, survived the war. I learned that he did and he emigrated to Paris. He operated an adding machine and typewriter factory there.

3.   I had to show my family my broken background—the evidence remaining at Dachau and other places. I took my wife and sons to Germany and walked them through Dachau and showed them the crematorium and gas chamber that

I feared so much. While in Europe, we also went to Paris to visit Mr. Wise. He was in Israel at the time and regretfully we did not get to see him.

4.   I had to go to Israel to visit my mother's side of the family. Her two brothers had already died. A few years ago, I took my wife to Israel to visit my cousins and also a friend of mine from Blyzin whom I had not seen in 43 years. It was a joyous reunion.

5.   The last thing I needed to do was to tell my story to those who are interested in history and the injustice of human oppression. It may serve as a warning to those who might allow it to happen again, through ignorance, if they do not learn of the reality of this Holocaust and its effect on the world. At the end there are no winners—only a path that we leave behind to be remembered by. Hitler and the SS will be remembered by their paths; others, like Churchill, Roosevelt, and the Allied soldiers will be remembered by theirs.

6.   I searched my soul since my liberation, May 5th 1945, *"Why me"*? For what reason had God chosen me, the youngest known survivor of the Holocaust from my city of 20,000 Jews?

The answers came to me in a dream one night. Three possibilities surfaced. Like a bolt of blue-white lightening, split open the most inner part of my subconscious that had remained deliberately locked for so many years. It was as clear to me as the bluest waters. I was almost angry with myself for not seeing the answers sooner:

I was saved to *tell the story* for all who were silenced by death and torture, gassed and burned, and can speak no more.

I was spared to let go of *anger, hatred, and resentment,* to help others do the same, so people could live a more productive and satisfying life in the future. I was *robbed of my youth, education, country, family and everything that was familiar and meaningful in my life.* If I could triumph over this great loss, **so can you!**

I feel compelled to give charity and under-standing to those who have not yet been able to find it in their hearts to set aside injustices, wrongdoings, hurts, infringements, and violations done to them in the past; to be "a light unto the nations," as it says in the Bible; so that the world may learn through my heartaches and triumphs!

If you were to ask me what the major accomplishments were in my life, I would have to say that there are only three which I consider major.

A. Putting aside the hatred for the Nazis that had been building in me while suffering in concentration camps for five long years and watching my entire family gassed and burned, living for the day I could take revenge. That extraordinary ability made everything else possible for me.

B. My successful marriage to Joyce for more than 41 years. She has been my best and most trusted friend. She has never asked for anything I couldn't give her. She has definitely been family oriented, serving as a moral guide for all of us to follow. Her heart is as big as the world and her greatest pleasure has been giving of herself to those she loves.

C. The third, and only because without the first two this would not be possible, was raising our two sons, of whom my wife and I are very proud. The older, Steven, is a successful attorney who is practicing law in our community. Our younger son, David, is in the insurance business and is also very successful in his endeavors.

Throughout our lives, we have served in various service organizations and have enjoyed giving of ourselves to a community that has been so good to us.

With our children grown, and while still in good health, Joyce and I are looking forward to seeing more of this country of ours in our mini motorhome. We want to see every state, every river, every nook and cranny. We also want to meet as many people along the way as we can. We want to honor all the people who have helped make this country great. We want to thank all of those who fought so hard to give us the opportunity to live in this great, blessed land! *WE WANT TO THANK THOSE WHO CAME BEFORE US AND PAVED THE WAY FOR FREEDOM OF RELIGION, EXPRESSION, AND FOR THE OPPORTUNITY TO EARN A DECENT LIVING, if one is willing to work for it. . . .*

Order Form

- Telephone orders .... (408) 422 4098
- Fax Orders .... (408) 422 4098

- Postal Orders: H & J Publishing Inc.
                   P.O. Box 2253
                   Salinas, Calif. 93902-2253

Bill TO:
Co. name: _____
Name: _____
Address: _____
City:_____State:___ Zip:_____Ph. ( )_____

SHIP TO:
Co. name _____
Name: _____
Address: _____
City: _____ State:_____ Zip: _____

Shipping & Handling:
Book rate $3.50.   Air Mail $4.90 ea.

Payment:
☐ Check   ☐ Visa   ☐ Master Card   ☐Am. Express
Card Number: _____
Name on Card _____Exp. Date____
Signature of Card Holder _____

Quan: ___ Hard Cover @ $25.95 .... $_____
Quan: ___ Soft Cover @ $15.95 .... $_____
Total Quan: _____ @ $3.50 or @ $4.90ea.... $_____
California Sales Tax: 7.75% .... $_____

Total .... $_____

This Order Form may be Reproduced